It's another Quality Book from CGP

This book is for anyone doing Edexcel Modular
GCSE Mathematics at Foundation Level.

It contains lots of tricky questions designed
to make you sweat — because that's the only
way you'll get any better.

It's also got some daft bits in to try and make
the whole experience at least vaguely
entertaining for you.

What CGP is all about

Our sole aim here at CGP is to produce the highest quality
books — carefully written, immaculately presented and
dangerously close to being funny.

Then we work our socks off to get them out to you
— at the cheapest possible prices.

Contents

Unit Three

Throughout the book, the more challenging questions are marked like this: **Q1**.

Published by Coordination Group Publications Ltd.
Illustrated by Ruso Bradley, Lex Ward and Ashley Tyson

Contributors:

Gill Allen

Margaret Carr

Barbara Coleman

JE Dodds

Mark Haslam

John Lyons

Gordon Rutter

Dave Williams

Philip Wood

Updated by:
Simon Little and Ali Palin

With thanks to Charley Darbishire *and*
Janet Dickinson *for the proofreading.*

ISBN: 978 1 84762 091 0

Groovy website: www.cgpbooks.co.uk

Printed by Elanders Hindson Ltd, Newcastle upon Tyne.
Clipart sources: CorelDRAW® and VECTOR.

Probability

When you're asked to find the probability of something, always check that your answer is between 0 and 1. If it's not, you know straight away that you've made a mistake.

Q1   Write down whether these events are impossible, unlikely, even, likely or certain.

   a) You will go shopping on Saturday. ....

   b) You will live to be 300 years old. ....

   c) The next person who comes into the room is female. ....

   d) There will be a moon in the sky tonight. ....

Q2   A bag contains ten balls. Five are red, three are yellow and two are green.
   What is the probability of picking out:

   a) A yellow ball? ....

   b) A red ball? ....

   c) A green ball? ....

   d) A red or a green ball? ....

   e) A blue ball? ....

Q3   Write down the probability of these events happening:

   a) Throwing an odd number with a six-sided dice. ....

   b) Drawing a black card from a pack of playing cards. ....

   c) Drawing a black King from a pack of cards. ....

   d) Throwing a prime number with a six-sided dice. ....

Q4   Mike and Nick play a game of pool. The probability of Nick winning is 7/10.

   a) Put an arrow on the probability line below to show the probability of Nick winning.
   Label this arrow N.

   b) Now put an arrow on the probability line to show the probability of Mike winning the
   game. Label this arrow M.

Probability

Q5 The outcome when a coin is tossed is head (H) or tail (T).
Complete this table of outcomes when two coins are tossed together.

    a) How many possible outcomes are there? ....

    b) What is the probability of getting 2 heads? ....

    c) What is the probability of getting a head
    followed by a tail? ....

		2nd COIN	
		H	**T**
1st COIN	**H**		
	T		

Q6 Two dice are rolled together. The scores on the dice are added.
Complete the table of possible outcomes below.

How many different combinations are there? ....

SECOND DICE						
FIRST DICE	**1**	**2**	**3**	**4**	**5**	**6**
1						
2	3					
3						
4						
5			8			
6						

What is the probability of scoring:

a) 2 ....

b) 6 ....

c) 10 ....

d) More than 9 ....

e) Less than 4 ....

f) An even number ....

g) More than 12 ....

Q7 Two spinners are spun and the scores are multiplied together.

		SPINNER 1		
		2	**3**	**4**
SPINNER 2	**3**			
	4			
	5			

Fill in this table of possible outcomes.

What is the probability of scoring 12? ....

To win you have to score 15 or more.
What is the probability of winning? ....

In the exam, you might not be asked to put the "possible outcomes" in a table. But it's a good idea to make your own table anyway — that way you don't miss any out.

Probability

Well, OK, the probability is that you'd rather not be doing these at all... still — this is the last page, so I'm sure you'll cope for a bit longer.

Q8 One day Sarah did a survey in her class on sock colour. She found out that pupils were wearing white socks, black socks or red socks. Jack said "If I pick someone at random from the class, then the probability that they are wearing red socks is 1/3." Explain why Jack might be wrong.

....

....

Q9 Imagine you have just made a 6-sided spinner in Design and Technology. How could you test whether or not it's a fair spinner?

....

Remember — if the spinner's fair, the probability of landing on each side is the same.

....

....

Q10 a) A biased dice is rolled 40 times. A six came up 14 times. Calculate the relative frequency that a six was rolled.

....

b) The same dice is rolled another 60 times. From this, a six came up 24 times. Calculate the relative frequency that a six was rolled.

....

c) Use the data from a) and b) to make the best estimate you can of the probability of rolling a six with the dice.

....

Q11 "There is a 50% chance that it will rain tomorrow because it will either rain or it won't rain." Is this statement true or false? Explain your answer.

....

....

....

Mode and Median

To find the mode, put the data in order of size first — then it's easier to see which number you've got most of.

Q1 Find the mode for each of these sets of data.

a) 3, 5, 8, 6, 3, 7, 3, 5, 3, 9,

.... Mode is ....

b) 52, 26, 13, 52, 31, 12, 26, 13, 52, 87, 41

.... Mode is ....

Q2 The temperature in °C on 10 Summer days in England was:

25, 18, 23, 19, 23, 24, 23, 18, 20, 19

What was the modal temperature?

.... Modal temperature is .... °C.

Q3 The time it takes thirty pupils in a class to get to school each day in minutes is:

18, 24, 12, 28, 17, 34, 17, 17, 28, 12, 23, 24, 17, 34, 9,
32, 15, 31, 17, 19, 17, 32, 15, 17, 21, 29, 34, 17, 12, 17

What is the modal time?

....

....

Modal time is .... mins.

Put the data in order of size for median questions too — it's much easier to find the middle value.

Q4 Find the median for these sets of data.

a) 3, 6, 7, 12, 2, 5, 4, 2, 9

.... Median is ....

b) 14, 5, 21, 7, 19, 3, 12, 2, 5

.... Median is ....

Q5 These are the heights of fifteen 16 year olds.

162 cm   156 cm   174 cm   148 cm   152 cm   139 cm   167 cm   134 cm
157 cm   163 cm   149 cm   134 cm   158 cm   172 cm   146 cm

What is the median height? Write your answer in the shaded box.

| | | | | | | | | | | | | Median |

Mean and Range

Yikes — MEAN questions... well, they're not as bad as everyone makes out. Remember to include zeros in your calculations — they still count.

Q1 Find the mean of each of the sets of data below. If necessary, round your answers to 1 decimal place:

a) 13, 15, 11, 12, 16, 13, 11, 9 = ...

b) 16, 13, 2, 15, 0, 9 = ...

> Remember the formula for mean —
> total of the items ÷ number of items.

c) 80, 70, 80, 50, 60, 70, 90, 60, 50, 70, 70 = ...

Q2 Find, <u>without</u> a calculator, the mean for each of these sets of data:

a) 5, 3, 7, 3, 2 = ...

b) 7, 3, 9, 5, 3, 5, 4, 6, 2, 6 = ...

Q3 **a)** Stephen scored a mean mark of 64 in four Maths tests. What was his total mark for all four tests?

....

b) When he did the next test, his mean mark went up to 66. What mark did he get in the fifth test?

....

Q4 The number of goals scored by a hockey team over a period of 10 games is listed below.

0, 3, 2, 4, 1, 2, 3, 4, 1, 0.

What is the range of the number of goals scored? ....

Q5 Sarah and her friends were measured and their heights were found to be:

1.52 m, 1.61 m, 1.49 m, 1.55 m, 1.39 m, 1.56 m.

What is the range of the heights? ....

Q6 Here are the times 6 people took to do a Maths test:

1 hour 10 mins, 2 hours 10 mins, 1 hour 35 mins,
1 hours 55 min, 1 hour 18 mins, 2 hours 15 mins.

What is the range of these times? ....

Averages

 Geesh — as if it's not enough to make you work out all these boring averages, they want you to write stuff about them as well. Oh well, here goes nothing.

Q1 These are the mathematics marks for John and Mark.

John	65	83	58	79	75
Mark	72	70	81	67	70

Calculate the mean and range for each pupil. Who do you think is the better maths student? Why?

....

....

Q2 Jane has a Saturday job. She earns £3.70 an hour. She thinks that most of her friends earn more. Here is a list of how much an hour her friends are paid.

Lisa £3.60   Scott £4.50   Kate £4.25   Kylie £3.40
Helen £4.01   Kirsty £4.25   Ben £4.25   Ruksana £3.90

Work out the mean, median and mode for her friends' pay.

....

....

Jane's employer offers her a rise to £4.02 because she claims that this is the average hourly rate. Which average has her employer used?

....

Which average should Jane use to try to negotiate a higher pay rise?

....

Q3 The number of absences for 20 pupils during the spring term were:

0 0 0 0 0 0 1 1 1 2 3 4 4 4 7 9 10 10 19 22

Work out the mean, median and modal number of absences.

....

....

If you were a local newspaper reporter wishing to show that the local school has a very poor attendance record, which average would you use and why?

....

If you were the head teacher writing a report for the parents of new pupils which average would you use and why?

....

Averages

Q4 On a large box of matches it says "Average contents 240 matches".
I counted the number of matches in ten boxes. These are the results:

241 244 236 240 239 242 237 239 239 236

Is the label on the box correct? Use the mean, median and mode for the numbers of matches to explain your answer.

....

....

Q5 The shoe sizes in a class of girls are:

3 3 4 4 5 5 5 5 6 6 6 7 8

Calculate the mean, median and mode for the shoe sizes.

....

....

If you were a shoe shop manager, which average would be most useful to you, and why?

....

Q6 A house-building company needs a bricklayer.
This advert appears in the local newspaper.
The company employs the following people:

Position	Wage
Director	£700
Foreman	£360
Plasterer	£300
Bricklayer	£250
Bricklayer	£250

What is the median wage?

....

What is the mean wage? ....

Which gives the best idea
of the average wage? ....

Is the advert fair? Explain your answer.

Write a fairer advert
in the space above.

....

8

Tally / Frequency Tables

Q1   At the British Motor Show 60 people were asked what type of car they preferred.
Jeremy wrote down their replies using a simple letter code.

Saloon - S   Hatchback - H   4x4 - F   MPV - M   Roadster - R

Here is the full list of replies.

H	S	R	S	S	R	M	F	S	S	R	R
M	H	S	H	R	H	M	S	F	S	M	S
R	R	H	H	H	S	M	S	S	R	H	H
H	H	R	R	S	S	M	M	R	H	M	H
H	S	R	F	F	R	F	S	M	S	H	F

Fill in the tally table and add up the frequency in
each row. Draw the frequency graph of the results.

A **frequency graph** just means a bar chart.

TYPE OF CAR	TALLY	FREQUENCY
Saloon		
Hatchback		
4 × 4		
MPV		
Roadster		

Q2   Last season Newcaster City played 32 matches.
The number of goals they scored in each match were recorded as shown.

2	4	3	5
1	0	3	2
4	2	1	2
0	2	3	1

1	0	0	1
1	1	1	0
1	3	2	0
1	1	0	4

Complete the tally chart and draw the frequency polygon of the goals.

A **frequency polygon** is
where you plot points for
the frequencies and join
them up with straight lines.

GOALS	TALLY	FREQUENCY
0		
1		
2		
3		
4		
5		

Tally / Frequency Tables

Q3 Here is a list of marks which 32 pupils gained in a History test:

65	78	49	72	38	59	63	44
55	50	60	73	66	54	42	72
33	52	45	63	65	51	70	68
84	61	42	58	54	64	75	63

Complete the tally table making sure you put each mark in the correct group.
Then fill in the frequency column.

MARKS	TALLY	FREQUENCY
31-40		
41-50		
51-60		
61-70		
71-80		
81-90		
	TOTAL	

Q4 The frequency table below shows the number of hours spent Christmas shopping by 100 people surveyed in a town centre.

Number of Hours	0	1	2	3	4	5	6	7	8
Frequency	1	9	10	10	11	27	9	15	8
Hours × Frequency									

a) What is the modal number of hours spent Christmas shopping? ....

b) Fill in the third row of the table.

c) What is the total amount of time spent Christmas shopping by all the people surveyed?

....

d) What is the mean amount of time spent Christmas shopping by a person?

....

Grouped Frequency Tables

 As a rule these are trickier than standard frequency tables — you'll certainly have to tread carefully here. Have a good look at the box below and make sure you remember it.

Mean and Mid-Interval Values

1) The <u>MID-INTERVAL VALUES</u> are just what they sound like — the middle of the group.

2) Using the Frequencies and Mid-Interval Values you can estimate the <u>MEAN</u>.

$$\text{Estimated Mean} = \frac{\text{Overall Total (Frequency} \times \text{Mid-interval value)}}{\text{Frequency total}}$$

Shoe Size	1 - 2	3 - 4	5 - 6	7 - 8	Totals
Frequency	15	10	3	1	29
Mid-Interval Value	1.5	3.5	5.5	7.5	—
Frequency x Mid-Interval Value	22.5	35	16.5	7.5	81.5

So the estimated mean value is 81.5 ÷ 29 = 2.81

Q1 In a survey of test results in a French class at Blugdon High, these grades were achieved by the 23 pupils:

(Grade) Score	(E) 31-40	(D) 41-50	(C) 51-60	(B) 61-70
Frequency	4	7	8	4

a) Write down the mid-interval values for each of the groups.

....

b) Calculate an estimate for the mean value.

....

....

Q2 This table shows times for each team of swimmers, the Dolphins and the Sharks.

Dolphins			Sharks		
Time interval (seconds)	Frequency	Mid-interval value	Time interval (seconds)	Frequency	Mid-interval value
14 ≤ t < 20	3	17	14 ≤ t < 20	6	17
20 ≤ t < 26	7	23	20 ≤ t < 26	15	23
26 ≤ t < 32	15		26 ≤ t < 32	33	
32 ≤ t < 38	32		32 ≤ t < 38	59	
38 ≤ t < 44	45		38 ≤ t < 44	20	
44 ≤ t < 50	30		44 ≤ t < 50	8	
50 ≤ t < 56	5		50 ≤ t < 56	2	

a) Complete the table, writing in all mid-interval values.

b) Use the mid-interval technique to estimate the mean time for each team.

....

....

Tables, Charts and Graphs

Q1 Here is a horizontal bar chart showing the favourite colours of a class of pupils.

    a) How many like blue best? ....

    b) How many more people chose red than yellow? ....

    c) How many pupils took part in this survey? ....

    d) What fraction of the class prefer green? ....

Q2 This bar chart shows the marks from a test done by some students:

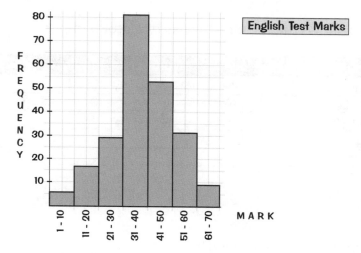

    a) How many students scored 20 marks or less? ....

    b) The pass mark for this test was 31. How many students passed the test? ....

    c) How many students took the test? ....

Q3 Complete this frequency table, and then draw a bar chart for the results.

TEST SCORE	TALLY	FREQUENCY
1 - 5	⊪⊩ I	6
6 - 10	⊪⊩ III	
11 - 15	III	
16 - 20	⊪⊩	
21 - 25	III	

UNIT ONE

Tables, Charts and Graphs

 Make sure you read these questions carefully. You don't want to lose easy marks by looking at the wrong bit of the table or chart.

Q4   One hundred people were asked in a survey what colour eyes they had.
Use this two-way table to answer the following questions.

a) How many people in the survey had green eyes? ....

b) How many women took part in the survey? ....

c) How many women had blue eyes? ....

d) How many men had brown eyes? ....

	Green eyes	Blue eyes	Brown eyes	Total
Male	15			48
Female	20		23	
Total		21		100

Q5   This pictogram shows the favourite drinks of a group of pupils.

Favourite Drinks	Number of Pupils
Lemonade	✧ ✧ ✧ ✧ ✧ ✧ ✧ ✧ ✧
Coke	✧ ✧ ✧ ✧ ✧ ✧ ✧ ✧ ✧ ✧
Tango	✧ ✧ ✧ ✧ ✧ ✧
Orange Squash	✧ ✧ ✧
Milk	✧

✧ Represents 2 pupils.

a) How many pupils were questioned? .... pupils.

b) How many pupils prefer non-fizzy drinks? .... pupils.

c) 18 pupils liked lemonade best. How many more liked coke best? .... pupils.

d) Comment on the popularity of coke compared with milk.

....

Q6   Carol was asked to find out if most people have a calculator in their Maths lessons.
She asked the people she liked in her Maths set if they had brought a calculator to
school. This table shows their responses:

Yes	No
II	III

From this she claims most people do not
have a calculator. Give 3 criticisms of Carol's survey.

....

....

Stem & Leaf Diagrams and Line Graphs

Q1 This stem and leaf diagram shows the ages of people in a cinema showing 'The Lord of The Things'.

```
1 | 2 2 4 8 8 9 9
2 | 0 1 1 2 5 6
3 | 0 0 0 5
4 | 2 5 9
5 |
6 | 8
```

Key: 2 | 5 means 25

a) How many people in the cinema were in their twenties? ....

b) Write out the ages of all of the people in the cinema below.

Q2 I've been measuring my friends' noses. Here are the lengths in millimetres:

    12   18   20   11   31
    19   27   34   19   22

Complete the stem and leaf diagram on the right to show the results above.

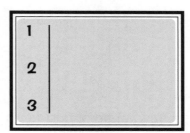

```
1 |
2 |
3 |
```

Key: 2 | 2 means 22

Q3 A baby was weighed every 5 days. The results are given below. Draw a line graph to show how the baby's weight changed.

DAY Nº	0	5	10	15	20	25	30
WEIGHT KG	5.3	5.2	5.9	6.4	6.6	6.7	6.8

In your own words describe how the baby's weight changed:

....

....

....

....

Scattergraphs

Q1 These are the shoe sizes and heights for 12 pupils in Year 11.

Shoe size	5	6	4	6	7	7	8	3	5	9	10	10
Height (cm)	155	157	150	159	158	162	162	149	152	165	167	172

On the grid below draw a scattergraph to show this information.

Draw a line of best fit on your scattergraph.

> A line of best fit goes through the middle of the points.

What does the scattergraph tell you about the relationship between shoe size and height for these pupils?

....

Q2 The scattergraphs below show the relationship between:

a) The temperature of the day and the amount of ice cream sold.
b) The price of ice cream and the amount sold.
c) The age of customers and the amount of ice cream sold.

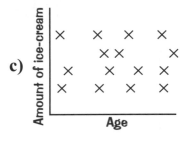

Describe the correlation of each graph and say what each graph tells you.

a)
....

b)
....

c)
....

Pie Charts

Q1 In a University department there are 180 students from different countries.

Country	UK	Malaysia	Spain	Others
Number of students	90	35	10	45

To show this on a Pie chart you have to work out the angle of each sector. Complete the table showing your working. The UK is done for you.

COUNTRY	WORKING	ANGLE in degrees
UK	90 ÷ 180 × 360 =	180°
MALAYSIA		
SPAIN		
OTHERS		

Now complete the Pie chart using an angle measurer. The UK sector is done for you.

Q2 This table shows the daily amount of air time of programme types on TV:

Programme	Hours	Angle
News	5	
Sport	3	
Music	2	
Current Affairs	3	
Comedy	2	
Other	9	
Total	24	

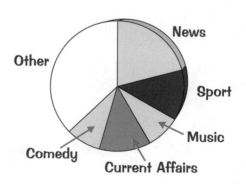

Complete the table by finding the size of the angle represented by each type of programme. Use an angle measurer or calculation method.

The full circle (that's all 360° of it) represents the total of everything — so you shouldn't find any gaps in it, basically.

Ordering Numbers and Place Value

Q1   Put these numbers in ascending (smallest to biggest) order.

a) 23   117   5   374   13   89   67   54   716   18

....

b) 1272   231   817   376   233   46   2319   494   73   1101

....

Q2   Write down the value of the number 4 in each of these.

For example   408   *hundreds*......

a) 347 ....

b) 41 ....

c) 5478 ....

d) 6754 ....

e) 4897 ....

f) 6045 ....

g) 64098 ....

h) 745320 ....

i) 405759 ....

j) 2402876 ....

k) 4987321 ....

l) 6503428 ....

Q3   Put these numbers in order of size — from the smallest to the largest.

a) 3.42   4.23   2.43   3.24   2.34   4.32

....

b) 6.700   6.704   6.640   6.642   6.741

....

> Always look at the whole number part first, then the first digit after the decimal point, then the next etc.

c) 1002.8   102.8   1008.2   1020.8   108.2

....

Multiplying by 10, 100, etc.

Multiplying by 10, 100 or 1000 moves each digit 1, 2 or 3 places
to the left — you just fill the rest of the space with zeros.

Fill in the missing numbers. Do not use a calculator for this page.

no calculators!!

Q1 **a)** $6 \times \boxed{} = 60$ **b)** $0.07 \times \boxed{} = 0.7$

c) $6 \times \boxed{} = 600$ **d)** $0.07 \times \boxed{} = 7$

e) $6 \times \boxed{} = 6000$ **f)** $0.07 \times \boxed{} = 70$

Q2 Which number is ten times as large as 25? ....

Q3 Which number is one hundred times as large as 93? ....

Q4 **a)** $8 \times 10 =$ .... **b)** $34 \times 100 =$ .... **c)** $52 \times 100 =$ ....

d) $9 \times 1000 =$ .... **e)** $436 \times 1000 =$ .... **f)** $0.2 \times 10 =$ ....

g) $6.9 \times 10 =$ .... **h)** $4.73 \times 100 =$ ....

Q5 For a school concert chairs are put out in rows of 10.
How many will be needed for 16 rows? ....

Q6   £2.99 EACH   How much do 10 chickens cost? ....

Q7 A school buys calculators for £2.45 each.
How much will 100 cost? ....

Q8   A shop bought 1000 bars of chocolate for £0.43 each.
How much did they cost altogether? ....

Q9 **a)** $20 \times 30 =$ .... **b)** $40 \times 700 =$ .... **c)** $250 \times 20 =$ ....

d) $6000 \times 210 =$ .... **e)** $18000 \times 500 =$ ....

Dividing by 10, 100, etc.

Dividing by 10, 100 or 1000 moves each digit 1, 2 or 3 places to the right.

Answer these questions <u>without</u> using a calculator:

Q1 **a)** 30 ÷ 10 = ... **b)** 43 ÷ 10 = ... **c)** 5.8 ÷ 10 = ...

d) 63.2 ÷ 10 = ... **e)** 0.5 ÷ 10 = ... **f)** 400 ÷ 100 = ...

g) 423 ÷ 100 = ... **h)** 228.6 ÷ 100 = ... **i)** 61.5 ÷ 100 = ...

j) 2.96 ÷ 100 = ... **k)** 6000 ÷ 1000 = ... **l)** 6334 ÷ 1000 = ...

m) 753.6 ÷ 1000 = ... **n)** 8.15 ÷ 1000 = ... **o)** 80 ÷ 20 = ...

p) 860 ÷ 20 = ... **q)** 2400 ÷ 300 = ... **r)** 480 ÷ 40 = ...

s) 860 ÷ 200 = ... **t)** 63.9 ÷ 30 = ...

Q2 Ten people share a Lottery win of £62.
How much should each person receive?

....

Q3 Blackpool Tower is 158 m tall. If a model
of it is built to a scale of 1 : 100, how tall
would the model be?

....

Millom

Q4 If 1000 identical ball-bearings weigh 2100 g,
what is the weight of one of the ball-bearings?

....

Q5 Mark went on holiday to France. He exchanged £200 for 320 euros to spend while
he was there. How many euros did he get for each £1?

....

Adding and Subtracting

 NO CALCULATORS HERE! ALWAYS put the numbers in **COLUMNS** when you're adding or subtracting... and check the **UNITS, TENS & HUNDREDS** line up.

Q1 Do these questions as quickly as you can:

a) 63
    +32

b) 75
    +48

c) 528
    +196

Q2 Now try these, writing the answers in the spaces provided:

a) 5 + 9

b) 26 + 15

c) 34 + 72

= ....

= ....

= ....

d) 238 + 56

e) 528 + 173

f) 215 + 2514

= ....

= ....

= ....

Q3 Subtract the following:

a) 36 – 13

b) 45 – 23

c) 89 – 24

= ....

= ....

= ....

d) 25 – 8

e) 80 – 42

f) 72 – 19

= ....

= ....

= ....

Q4 Scafell Pike is 979 m high. Ben Nevis is 1344 m high.
What is the difference in height between the two mountains?

The word 'difference' tells you it's a subtraction question.

Q5 Fill in the missing digits:

a)   6 5
    −3 •
    ─────
     • 4

b)   7 3 •
    −2 • 4
    ─────
     • 2 5

c)   8 7 •
    − • 3 2
    ─────
     2 • 9

d)   • 5 6
    −2 7 8
    ─────
     1 • •

Adding and Subtracting Decimals

Q1   Work out the answers without using a calculator.

    a)   2.4
          +3.2

    b)   3.5
          +4.6

    c)   6.2
          +5.9

    d)   7.34
          +6.07

    e)   9.08
          +4.93

    f)   1 5.73
          +25.08

    g)   26.05
          +72.95

Q2   Write these out in columns and work out the answer without using a calculator.

    a) 3.6 + 7.3   **b)** 21.4 + 13.8   **c)** 0.9 + 5.6   **d)** 9.98 + 6.03   **e)** 2.9 + 7

    f) 4.36 + 7.1   **g)** 9.8 + 1.05   **h)** 6 + 6.75   **i)** 0.28 + 18.5   **j)** 47.23 + 6.7

Q3   Work these out <u>without</u> a calculator:

    a)   9.8
          −3.1

    b)   7.3
          −2.3

    c)   6.2
          − 1.5

    d)   8.6
          − 3.9

    e)   7.0
          −1.6

    f)   13.6
          −12.7

    g)   14.65
          − 4.7

    h)   8.34
          − 4.65

Q4   Put the following in columns first, then work them out without using a calculator:

    a) 8.5 − 1.6   **b)** 18.3 − 5.9   **c)** 24.1 − 16.3

You have to give the whole numbers a decimal point yourself... and some zeros too. E.g. 9 − 3.6 becomes 9.0 − 3.6.

    d) 9 − 3.6   **e)** 40 − 2.3   **f)** 51 − 18.32

Multiplying

Q1   Multiply the following <u>without</u> a calculator:

a) 23 × 2

b) 40 × 3

c) 53 × 4

= ....

= ....

= ....

d) 13 × 5

e) 25 × 4

f) 42 × 3

= ....

= ....

= ....

g)   18 × 2   **h)**   54 × 3   **i)**   75 × 5   **j)**   93 × 4

= ....

= ....

= ....

= ....

k)   308 × 4   **l)**   825 × 3   **m)**   346 × 5   **n)**   286 × 6

= ....

= ....

= ....

= ....

o)   126 × 14   **p)**   413 × 26   **q)**   309 × 61   **r)**   847 × 53

= ....

= ....

= ....

= ....

Q2   Without using a calculator, work out the total cost of 6 pens at 54p each.

....

Q3   Without using a calculator, calculate how many hours there are in a year (365 days).

....

Dividing

Do these division questions <u>without</u> a calculator:

Q1 **a)** 46 ÷ 2   You may wish to set the sum out like this

$$2\overline{)\,46\,}^{\,23}$$

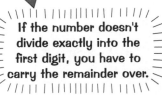

b) 86 ÷ 2   **c)** 96 ÷ 3   **d)** 76 ÷ 4

If the number doesn't divide exactly into the first digit, you have to carry the remainder over.

e) 85 ÷ 5   **f)** 96 ÷ 6   **g)** 91 ÷ 7

Q2   Try these:

a) 834 ÷ 3   **b)** 645 ÷ 5   **c)** 702 ÷ 6

d) 900 ÷ 4   **e)** 1000 ÷ 8   **g)** 747 ÷ 9

Q3   Seven people share a lottery win of £868.00. How much did each person get?

....

Q4   A chocolate cake containing 944 calories is split into 8 slices.
How many calories are in each slice?

....

Multiplying Decimals

A good way to multiply decimals is to ignore the decimal point to start with — just multiply the numbers. Then put the point back in and **CHECK** your answer looks sensible.

Do these calculations <u>without</u> using a calculator:

Q1 **a)** 3.2 × 4 **b)** 8.3 × 5 **c)** 6.4 × 3

= .... = ... = ...

d) 21 × 0.3 **e)** 263 × 0.2 **f)** 2.4 × 3.1

= .... = ... = ...

Q2 At a petrol station each pump shows a ready reckoner table. Complete the table when the cost of unleaded petrol is 94.9p per litre.

Litres	Cost in pence
1	94.9
5	
10	
20	
50	

Q3 Jason can run 5.3 metres in 2 seconds. How far will he run if he keeps up this pace for:

a) 20 seconds **b)** 60 seconds **c)** 5 minutes

....

Carl can run 7.4 metres in 2 seconds. How far will he run if he keeps up this pace for:

d) 20 seconds **e)** 60 seconds **f)** 5 minutes

....

g) If they both keep up their pace for half an hour how far will each of them run?

Jason will run .... metres.

Carl will run .... metres.

Dividing Decimals

This is the same thing, really — you divide the numbers first,
then you put in the point where it should be.

Q1 Divide these without a calculator.

a) 8.4 ÷ 2   You may wish to set the sum out like this $2\overline{\smash{)}8.4}$ with 4.2 above

b) 7.5 ÷ 3   **c)** 8.5 ÷ 5   **d)** 26.6 ÷ 7

e) 6.2 ÷ 5   **f)** 2.3 ÷ 4   **g)** 0.9 ÷ 5

Q2 Try these without a calculator:

a) 2.06 ÷ 8   **b)** 0.405 ÷ 6   **c)** 0.3 ÷ 8

d) 4.75 ÷ 5   **e)** 8.28 ÷ 9   **f)** 0.944 ÷ 8

No calculators allowed for these two either:

Q3 Eight people share £9.36 equally. How much does each get?

....

Q4 A plank of wood 8.34 m long is cut into 6 equal pieces.
How long is each piece?

....

UNIT TWO

Rounding Off

Q1   Round the following to the nearest whole number:

a) 2.9 ....   **b)** 26.8 ....   **c)** 2.24 ....

d) 11.11 ....   **e)** 6.347 ....   **f)** 43.5 ....

g) 9.99 ....   **h)** 0.41 ....

> Nearest <u>whole number</u> means you look at the digit after the decimal point to decide whether to round up or down.

Q2   An average family has 2.3 children, how many children is this to the nearest whole number?

....

Q3   By the time she is 25 the average woman will have driven 4.72 cars. What is this to the nearest whole number?

....

Q4   Give these amounts to the nearest pound:

a) £4.29 ....   **b)** £16.78 ....   **c)** £12.06 ....

d) £7.52 ....   **e)** £0.93 ....   **f)** £14.50 ....

g) £7.49 ....   **h)** £0.28 ....

Q5   Give these amounts to the nearest hour:

a) 2 hours 12 minutes ....   **b)** 36 minutes ....

c) 12 hours 12 minutes ....   **d)** 29 minutes ....

e) 100 minutes ....   **f)** 90 minutes ....

Rounding Off

Q6   Round off these numbers to the nearest 10:

a) 23 ....   b) 78 ....   c) 65 ....   d) 99 ....

e) 118 ....   f) 243 ....   g) 958 ....   h) 1056 ....

Q7   Round off these numbers to the nearest 100:

a) 627 ....   b) 791 ....   c) 199 ....   d) 450 ....

e) 1288 ....   f) 3329 ....   g) 2993 ....

Q8   Round these off to the nearest 1000:

a) 5200 ....   b) 8860 ....   c) 9870 ....

Q9   Crowd sizes at sports events are often given exactly in newspapers. Round off these exact crowd sizes to the nearest 1000:

a) 23324 ....

b) 36844 ....

c) 49752 ....

Q10   The number of drawing pins in the box has been rounded to the nearest 10.

DRAWING PINS
Contents: 80

What is the least possible number of drawing pins in the box?   ....

What is the greatest possible number?   ....

Q11   The population of Whichtown is given as 1300 to the nearest 100. What is the smallest number the population could be?

....

What is the largest it could be?

....

When you round numbers off to the nearest unit, the ACTUAL measurement could be up to HALF A UNIT bigger or smaller...

Rounding Off

Q12   Round off these numbers to 1 decimal place (1 d.p.):

a) 7.34 ....   **b)** 8.47 ....   **c)** 12.08 ....   **d)** 28.03 ....

e) 9.35 ....   **f)** 14.618 ....   **g)** 30.409 ....

Q13   Round off the following to 2 d.p.

a) 17.363 ....   **b)** 38.057 ....   **c)** 0.735 ....

d) 5.99823 ....   **e)** 4.297 ....   **f)** 7.0409 ....

Q14   Now round these to 3 d.p.

a) 6.3534 ....   **b)** 81.64471 ....   **c)** 0.0075 ....

d) 53.26981 ....   **e)** 754.39962 ....   **f)** 0.000486 ....

Q15   Seven people have a meal in a restaurant. The total
bill comes to £60. If they share the bill equally,
how much should each of them pay?
Round your answer to 2 d.p.

....

Q16   Round these numbers to 1 significant figure.

a) 12   ....   **b)** 530   ....

c) 1379   ....   **d)** 0.021   ....

e) 1829.62   ....   **f)** 0.296   ....

The 1st significant figure of any number is the first digit which isn't zero.

Q17   At a golf club, a putting green is given as being 500 cm long to
1 significant figure. Give the range of values that the actual
length of the green could be.

....

Estimating

Q1   Estimate the answers to these questions…

For example: 12 × 21   <u>10 × 20 = 200</u>

a) 18 × 12   ……… × ……… = ………   **b)** 23 × 21   ……… × ……… = ………

c) 57 × 46   ……… × ……… = ………   **d)** 98 × 145   ……… × ……… = ………

e) 11 ÷ 4   ……… ÷ ……… = ………   **f)** 22 ÷ 6   ……… ÷ ……… = ………

g) 97 ÷ 9   ……… ÷ ……… = ………   **h)** 147 ÷ 14   ……… ÷ ……… = ………

i) 195 × 205   ……… × ……… = ………   **j)** 545 × 301   ……… × ……… = ………

k) 901 ÷ 33   ……… ÷ ……… = ………   **l)** 1207 ÷ 598   ……… ÷ ……… = ………

Q2   Write in the estimates that give the answer shown.

For example: 101 × 96   <u>100 × 100 = 10000</u>

a) 34 × 19   ……… × ……… = 600   **b)** 27 × 32   ……… × ……… = 900

c) 67 × 89   ……… × ……… = 6300   **d)** 99 × 9   ……… × ……… = 1000

e) 56 ÷ 11   ……… ÷ ……… = 6   **f)** 119 ÷ 17   ……… ÷ ……… = 6

g) 182 ÷ 62   ……… ÷ ……… = 3   **h)** 317 ÷ 81   ……… ÷ ……… = 4

Q3   Andy earns £12,404 a year. Bob earns £58,975 a year. Chris earns £81,006 a year.

a) Estimate how much Andy will earn over 3 years.   £ ………………

b) Estimate how many years Andy will have to work to earn
as much as Chris does in one year.   ………………

c) Estimate how much Bob earns per month.   £ ………………

**Round off to NICE EASY CONVENIENT NUMBERS,
then use them to do the sum. Easy peasy.**

Estimating

Q4   Estimate the following lengths then measure them to see how far out you were:

OBJECT	ESTIMATE	ACTUAL LENGTH
a) Length of your pen or pencil	....	....
b) Width of your thumbnail	....	....
c) Height of this page	....	....
d) Height of the room you are in	....	....

Q5

The ranger is almost 2 m tall. Estimate the height of the giraffe in metres.

....

If you have trouble estimating the height by eye, try measuring the ranger against your finger. Then see how many times that bit of finger fits into the height of the giraffe.

Q6   The distance from A to B is 50 km. Estimate the distance from A to C.

AC = ... km

• **A**   **B**•

                                    •**C**

Prime Numbers

Basically, prime numbers don't divide by anything (except 1 and themselves).
5 is prime — it will only divide by 1 or 5. 1 is an exception to this rule — it is not prime.

Q1   Write down the first ten prime numbers. ....

Q2   Give a reason for 27 not being a prime number. ....

Q3   Using any or all of the figures **1, 2, 3, 7** write down:

   a) the smallest prime number ....

   b) a prime number greater than 20 ....

   c) a prime number between 10 and 20 ....

   d) two prime numbers whose sum is 20 .... , ...

   e) a number that is not prime. ....

Q4   Find all the prime numbers between 40 and 50. ....

Q5   In the <u>ten by ten square</u> opposite,
ring all the prime numbers.

   The first three have been done for you.

1	②	③	4	⑤	6	7	8	9	10
11	12	13	14	15	16	17	18	19	20
21	22	23	24	25	26	27	28	29	30
31	32	33	34	35	36	37	38	39	40
41	42	43	44	45	46	47	48	49	50
51	52	53	54	55	56	57	58	59	60
61	62	63	64	65	66	67	68	69	70
71	72	73	74	75	76	77	78	79	80
81	82	83	84	85	86	87	88	89	90
91	92	93	94	95	96	97	98	99	100

Q6   A school ran three evening classes: <u>judo, karate and kendo</u>.
The judo class had 29 pupils, the karate class had 27 and the kendo class 23.
For which classes would the teacher have difficulty dividing the pupils into equal groups?

   ....

Q7   Find three sets of three prime numbers which add up to the following numbers:

   10 ...., ..., ...   **29** ...., ..., ...   **41** ...., ..., ...

Multiples

The multiples of a number are its times table — if you need multiples of more than one number, do them separately then pick the ones in both lists.

Q1   What are the first five multiples of:

a) 4? ....

b) 7? ....

c) 12? ....

d) 18? ....

Q2   Find a number which is a multiple of:

A quick way to do these is just to multiply the numbers together.

a) 2 and 6 ....

b) 7 and 5 ....

c) 2 and 3 and 7 ....

d) 4 and 5 and 9 ....

Q3 **a)** Find a number which is a multiple of 3 and 8 ....

b) Find another number which is a multiple of 3 and 8 ....

c) Find another number which is a multiple of 3 and 8 ....

Q4   Which of these numbers 14, 20, 22, 35, 50, 55, 70, 77, 99 are multiples of:

a) 2? ....

b) 5? ....

c) 7? ....

d) 11? ....

Factors

Q1 **a)** I am a factor of 24.
I am an odd number.
I am bigger than 1.
What number am I?

....

b) I am a factor of 30.
I am an even number.
I am less than 5.
What number am I?

....

Q2 Circle all the factors of 360 in this list of numbers.

1   2   3   4   5   6   7   8   9   10

Q3 A perfect number is one where the factors add up to the number itself.
For example, the factors of 28 are 1, 2, 4, 7 and 14 (not including 28 itself).
These add up to 1 + 2 + 4 + 7 + 14 = 28, and so 28 is a perfect number.

Complete this table, and circle the perfect number in the left hand column.

Number	Factors (excluding the number itself)	Sum of Factors
2		
4	1, 2	3
6		
8		
10		

The sum of the factors is all the factors added together.

Q4 **a)** What is the biggest number that is a factor of both 42 and 18?

....

b) What is the smallest number that has both 4 and 18 as factors?

....

Q5 Complete the factor trees below to express each number as a product of prime factors.
The first one has been done for you.

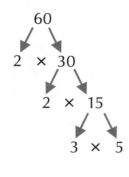

60

2 × 30

2 × 15

3 × 5

60 = 2×2×3×5

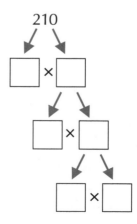

88

2 × □

2 × □

□ × □

210

□ × □

□ × □

□ × □

88 = 2×2×........×........   210 = ... ×........×........×........

LCM and HCF

The Lowest Common Multiple (LCM) is the **SMALLEST** number that will **DIVIDE BY ALL** the numbers in question.

The Highest Common Factor (HCF) is the **BIGGEST** number that will **DIVIDE INTO ALL** the numbers in question.

Q1 **a)** List the <u>first ten</u> multiples of 6, <u>starting at 6</u>.

....

b) List the <u>first ten</u> multiples of 5, <u>starting at 5</u>.

....

c) What is the <u>LCM</u> of 5 and 6?

....

Q2 For each set of numbers find the HCF.

a) 3, 5   **c)** 10, 15   **e)** 14, 21

....

b) 6, 8   **d)** 27, 48   **f)** 11, 33, 121

....

Q3 For each set of numbers, find the LCM.

a) 3, 5   **c)** 10, 15   **e)** 14, 21

....

b) 6, 8   **d)** 15, 18   **f)** 11, 33, 44

....

Q4 Lars, Rita and Alan regularly go swimming. Lars goes every 2 days, Rita goes every 3 days and Alan goes every 5 days. They <u>all</u> went swimming together on Friday 1st June.

This is a LCM question in disguise.

a) On what <u>date</u> will Lars and Rita next go swimming together?

....

b) On what <u>date</u> will Rita and Alan next go swimming together?

....

c) On what <u>day of the week</u> will all 3 next go swimming together?

....

d) Which of the 3 (if any) will go swimming on 15th June?

....

Fractions

  This circle is divided into two equal parts — each bit is 1/2 of the whole.

Q1 What fraction is shaded in each of the following pictures?

a)

....

b)

....

c)

....

d)

....

e)

....

f)

....

g)

....

Q2 Shade the diagram to show the following fractions.

a) $\frac{3}{8}$

b) $\frac{2}{5}$

c) $\frac{7}{10}$

Q3 There are 32 boxes of shoes stacked on a shelf.

If five eighths are sold, show on the diagram how many are left.

Fractions

To make an **EQUIVALENT** fraction, you've got to multiply the **TOP** (numerator) and **BOTTOM** (denominator) by the **SAME THING**.

Q4   Shade in the correct number of sections to make these diagrams equivalent.

Q5   Write in the missing numbers to make these fractions equivalent.

For example 1/2 = 7/14

a) 1/4 = 4/........   b) 3/4 = 9/........   c) 1/3 = ... /6

d) 2/3 = 8/........   e) 2/7 = 6/........   f) 6/18 = 1/........

g) 8/16 = ... /2   h) 24/32 = 3/........   i) 10/60 = 5/........

Q6   Write in the missing numbers to make each list equivalent.

a) 1/2 = 2/...... = ... /6 = ... /8 = 5/10 = 25/...... = ... /70 = ... /100

b) 200/300 = 100/...... = ... /15 = 40/...... = 120/180 = ... /9 = ... /3

c) 7/10 = 14/...... = ... /30 = 210/...... = 49/...... = ... /20

d) 19/20 = ... /80 = 38/...... = 57/...... = ... /100 = ... /1000

e) 500/600 = 250/...... = 50/...... = ... /150 = 1000/......

Q7   Which is bigger?

a) 1/5 or 2/10 ....   b) 3/7 or 6/21 ....

c) 10/15 or 4/6 ....   d) 1/3 or 33/100 ....

UNIT TWO

Fractions, Decimals, %

Q1   Change these fractions to decimals:

     a) $\dfrac{1}{2}$ ....   **b)** $\dfrac{3}{4}$ ....   **c)** $\dfrac{7}{10}$ ....   **d)** $\dfrac{19}{20}$ ....

     e) $\dfrac{1}{100}$ ....   **f)** $\dfrac{3}{8}$ ....   **g)** $\dfrac{2}{1000}$ ....   **h)** $\dfrac{1}{3}$ ....

Q2   Change these fractions to percentages:

     a) $\dfrac{1}{4}$ ....   **b)** $\dfrac{3}{10}$ ....   **c)** $\dfrac{4}{5}$ ....   **d)** $\dfrac{12}{25}$ ....

     e) $\dfrac{8}{100}$ ....   **f)** $\dfrac{2}{40}$ ....   **g)** $\dfrac{7}{8}$ ....   **h)** $\dfrac{11}{30}$ ....

Q3   Change these decimals to percentages:

     a) 0.62 ....   **b)** 0.74 ....   **c)** 0.4 ....   **d)** 0.9 ....

     e) 0.07 ....   **f)** 0.02 ....   **g)** 0.125 ....   **h)** 0.987 ....

Q4   Change these percentages to decimals:

     a) 25% ....   **b)** 49% ....   **c)** 3% ....   **d)** 30% ....

Q5   Change these percentages to fractions (in their lowest terms):

     a) 75% ....   **b)** 60% ....   **c)** 15% ....   **d)** 53% ....

Q6   Change these decimals to fractions (in their lowest terms):

     a) 0.5 ....   **b)** 0.8 ....   **c)** 0.19 ....   **d)** 0.25 ....

     e) 0.64 ....   **f)** 0.06 ....   **g)** 0.125 ....   **h)** 0.075 ....

A FRACTION IS A DECIMAL IS A PERCENTAGE —
they're all just different ways of saying "a bit of" something.

Powers

Q1 Complete the following:

a) $2^4 = 2 \times 2 \times 2 \times 2 = $ ....

b) $10^3 = 10 \times 10 \times 10 = $ ....

c) $3^5 = 3 \times$ .... $= $ ....

d) $4^6 = 4 \times$ .... $= $ ....

e) $1^9 = 1 \times$ .... $= $ ....

f) $5^6 = 5 \times$ .... $= $ ....

Q2 Simplify the following:

a) $2 \times 2 \times 2 \times 2 \times 2 \times 2 \times 2 \times 2 = $ ....

b) $12 \times 12 \times 12 \times 12 \times 12 = $ ....

c) $m \times m \times m = $ ....

d) $y \times y \times y \times y = $ ....

Q3 Use your <u>calculator</u> to find the exact value of

a) 4^3 .... **b)** 10^4 .... **c)** 12^5 .... **d)** 13^3 ....

Q4 Complete the following (the first one has been done for you):

a) $10^2 \times 10^3 = $ $(10 \times 10) \times (10 \times 10 \times 10)$ $= 10^5$

b) $10^3 \times 10^4 = $ .... $= $

c) $10^4 \times 10^2 = $ .... $= $

d) What is the <u>quick method</u> for writing down the final result in **b)** and **c)**?

....

Q5 Complete the following (the first one has been done for you):

a) $2^4 \div 2^2 = \dfrac{(2 \times 2 \times 2 \times 2)}{(2 \times 2)} = 2^2$

c) $4^5 \div 4^3 = \dfrac{(4 \times 4 \times 4 \times 4 \times 4)}{.....................} = $ ....

b) $2^5 \div 2^2 = \dfrac{(2 \times 2 \times 2 \times 2 \times 2)}{(2 \times 2)} = $ ....

d) $8^5 \div 8^2 = \dfrac{.....................}{.....................} = $ ....

e) What is the quick method for writing down the final result in **b)**, **c)** and **d)**?

....

<u>You can always write out all the 10s or whatever if you get stuck.</u>

Q6 Write the following as a <u>single term</u>:

a) $10^6 \div 10^4 = $ ....

b) $(8^2 \times 8^5) \div 8^3 = $ ....

c) $6^{10} \div (6^2 \times 6^3) = $ ....

d) $x^2 \times x^3 = $ ....

e) $a^5 \times a^4 = $ ....

f) $p^4 \times p^5 \times p^6 = $ ....

Powers are just a way of writing numbers in shorthand — they come in especially handy with big numbers. Imagine writing out 2^{138} — $2 \times 2 \times... \times 2 \times... \times 2 \times$ yawn $\times$ zzz...

UNIT TWO

Square and Cube Roots

Square root just means "WHAT NUMBER TIMES ITSELF (i.e. 2×2) GIVES..."
The square roots of 64 are 8 and –8 because 8×8=64 and -8×-8=64.

Cube root means "WHAT NUMBER TIMES ITSELF TWICE (i.e. 2×2×2) GIVES ..."
The cube root of 27 is 3 because 3×3×3=27.

Square roots always have a + and – answer, cube roots only have 1 answer.

Q1 Use the $\sqrt{}$ button on your calculator to find the following <u>positive</u> square roots to the nearest whole number.

a) $\sqrt{60}$ = ...   e) $\sqrt{520}$ = ...   i) $\sqrt{170}$ = ...

b) $\sqrt{19}$ = ...   f) $\sqrt{75}$ = ...   j) $\sqrt{7220}$ = ...

c) $\sqrt{34}$ = ...   g) $\sqrt{750}$ = ...   k) $\sqrt{1000050}$ = ...

d) $\sqrt{200}$ = ...   h) $\sqrt{0.9}$ = ...   l) $\sqrt{27}$ = ...

Q2 Without using a calculator, write down both answers to each of the following:

a) $\sqrt{4}$ = ...   d) $\sqrt{49}$ = ...   g) $\sqrt{144}$ = ...

b) $\sqrt{16}$ = ...   e) $\sqrt{25}$ = ...   h) $\sqrt{64}$ = ...

c) $\sqrt{9}$ = ...   f) $\sqrt{100}$ = ...   i) $\sqrt{81}$ = ...

Q3 Use your calculator to find the following:

a) $\sqrt[3]{4096}$ = ...   d) $\sqrt[3]{1000000}$ = ...

b) $\sqrt[3]{1728}$ = ...   e) $\sqrt[3]{1}$ = ...

c) $\sqrt[3]{1331}$ = ...   f) $\sqrt[3]{0.125}$ = ...

Q4 Without using a calculator, find the value of the following:

a) $\sqrt[3]{64}$ = ...   d) $\sqrt[3]{1000}$ = ...

b) $\sqrt[3]{512}$ = ...   e) $\sqrt[3]{216}$ = ...

c) $\sqrt[3]{125}$ = ...   f) $\sqrt[3]{8000}$ = ...

Q5 A square rug has an area of 400 m². What is the length of an edge?

....

Q6 A solid cube puzzle has a volume of 343 cm³. Find the length of one of its edges.

....

Standard Index Form

Writing very big (or very small) numbers gets a bit messy with all those zeros. That's if you don't use this standard index form. But, of course, the main reason for knowing about standard form is...you guessed it — it's in the Exam.

Any numbers written in Standard Index Form <u>always</u> look like:

This number must be between 1 and 10 but never equal to 10

$$a \times 10^n$$

This number is equal to the number of places the decimal point moves. n is +ve for larger numbers n is -ve for small numbers

eg.

$$580000000000000000 = 5.8 \times 10^{17}$$
$$43000000000000000000 = 4.3 \times 10^{19}$$
$$0.0000000000000017 = 1.7 \times 10^{-15}$$
$$0.00000000000000008 = 8 \times 10^{-17}$$

Q1 Complete the two tables below.

Number	Standard form
4500000000	
19300000000000	
	8.2×10^{12}
82000000	
	6.34×10^{8}
	4.02×10^{6}
423400000000	
	8.431×10^{7}
	1.03×10^{5}
4700	

Number	Standard form
0.000000006	
0.00000000072	
	8.5×10^{-6}
0.000000143	
	7.12×10^{-5}
	3.68×10^{-10}
	4.003×10^{-8}
0.0000009321	
	5.2×10^{-3}
	9.999×10^{-7}
0.00000000802	
	2.3104×10^{-6}
0.000001	

Q2 Find the value of the following, giving your answers in <u>standard form</u>.

a) $46 \times 4.2 \times 5000 =$ ....

d) $5000 \div 0.02 =$ ....

b) $20 \times 40 \times 50 \times 8.2 =$ ....

e) $62000 \div 0.31 =$ ....

c) $0.2 \times 0.3 \times 0.5 \times 0.1 =$ ....

f) $40000000 \div 1000 =$ ....

Standard Index Form

Q3 Rewrite the following, either in standard form or by
changing standard form to normal numbers.

a) Mercury is 694000000 km from the Sun.

....

b) The Sahara desert covers 8600000 km^2.

....

c) The Earth is approximately 4.5×10^9 years old.

....

d) The average depth of the Atlantic is 3.7×10^3 metres.

....

e) The charge on an electron is 1.6×10^{-19} Coulombs.

....

f) A Uranium nucleus can release 3.20×10^{-11} Joules of energy.

....

g) In Chemistry, Avogadro's constant is 6.033×10^{23}.

....

h) The length of the Earth's equator is 40076 km.

....

i) The population of the USA is approximately 249231000 people.

....

j) From Washington to Tokyo is 6763 miles.

....

k) A tonne of coal can produce 2.8×10^{10} Joules of energy.

....

l) The radius of the nucleus of an atom is 0.0000000000003 cm.

....

You've got to remember the formula $a \times 10^n$. To find n, count the number of spaces
the decimal point moves. If the number you're converting is large, n is positive. If it's
small, n is negative. And don't forget, a has to be between 1 and 10. Easy as cake...

Negative Numbers

Q1 Write these numbers in the correct position on the number line below:

a) −4   3   2   −3   −5   1

0

b) Which temperature is lower (colder), 8 °C or −4 °C ?   ....

c) Which temperature is 1° warmer than −24 °C ?   ....

Put the correct symbol, < or >, between the following pairs of numbers:

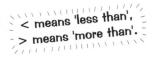
< means 'less than'.
> means 'more than'.

d) 4   −8

e) −6   −2

f) −8   −7

g) −3   −6

h) −1   1

i) −3.6   −3.7

j) Rearrange the following numbers in order of size, largest first:

   −2   2   0.5   −1.5   −8   ....

k) If the temperature is 6 °C but it then gets colder and falls by 11 °C, what is the new temperature?

   ....

l) One day in winter the temperature at 0600 was −9 °C. By midday, it had risen to −1 °C. By how many degrees did the temperature rise?

   ....

Always draw a number line to count along, so you can see what you're doing.

Negative Numbers

When you've got really big numbers, drawing a number line will still help. But just mark off the tens (or even just the hundreds) — you'll be there all day otherwise.

Answer these questions <u>without</u> using your calculator.

Q2   Work out:

a) $2 - 7 =$ ....

b) $4 - 18 =$ ....

c) $1 - 20 =$ ....

d) $12 - 14 =$ ....

e) $72 - 77 =$ ....

f) $3 - 100 =$ ....

Q3   Work out:

a) $-6 + 1 =$ ....

b) $-10 + 2 =$ ....

c) $-8 + 8 =$ ....

d) $-70 + 3 =$ ....

e) $-100 + 13 =$ ....

f) $-1000 + 1 =$ ....

Q4   Work out:

a) $-2 + 5 =$ ....

b) $-6 + 10 =$ ....

c) $-2 + 50 =$ ....

d) $-12 + 100 =$ ....

e) $-47 + 56 =$ ....

f) $-49 + 98 =$ ....

Q5   Work out:

a) $-3 - 2 =$ ....

b) $-3 - 6 =$ ....

c) $-13 - 3 =$ ....

d) $-50 - 4 =$ ....

e) $-2 - 19 =$ ....

f) $-7 - 96 =$ ....

Algebra — Collecting Terms and Expanding

Algebra can be pretty scary at first. But don't panic — the secret is just to practise lots and lots of questions. Eventually you'll be able to do it without thinking, just like riding a bike. But a lot more fun, obviously...

Simplifying means collecting _like terms_ together:	_Expanding_ means removing brackets:
$8x^2 + 2x + 4x^2 - x + 4$ becomes $12x^2 + x + 4$ x^2 term x term x^2 term x term number term	Eg $4(x + y) = 4x + 4y$ $x(2 + x) = 2x + x^2$ $-(a + b) = -a - b$

Q1 By collecting like terms, simplify the following.

a) $6x + 3x - 5 = 9x - 5$

b) $2x + 3x - 5x = $ ....

c) $9f + 16f + 15 - 30 = $ ....

d) $14x + 12x - 1 + 2x = $ ....

e) $3x + 4y + 12x - 5y = $ ....

f) $11a + 6b + 24a + 18b = $ ....

g) $9f + 16g - 15f - 30g = $ ....

h) $14a + 12a^2 - 3 + 2a = $ ....

Q2 Simplify the following:

a) $3x^2 + 5x - 2 + x^2 - 3x = 4x^2 + 2x - 2$

b) $5x^2 + 3 + 3x - 4 = $ ....

c) $13 + 2x^2 - 4x + x^2 + 5 = $ ....

d) $7y - 4 + 6y^2 + 2y - 1 = $ ....

e) $2a + 4a^2 - 6a - 3a^2 + 4 = $ ....

f) $15 - 3x - 2x^2 - 8 - 2x - x^2 = $ ....

g) $x^2 + 2x + x^2 + 3x + x^2 + 4x = $ ....

h) $2y^2 + 10y - 7 + 3y^2 - 12y + 1 = $ ....

Q3 Expand the brackets and then simplify if possible:

> Careful with the minus signs — they multiply both terms in the bracket.

a) $2(x + y) = 2x + 2y$

b) $4(x - 3) = $ ....

c) $8(x^2 + 2) = $ ....

d) $-2(x + 5) = $ ....

e) $-(y - 2) = $ ....

f) $x(y + 2) = $ ....

g) $x(x + y + z) = $ ....

h) $8(a + b) + 2(a + 2b) = $ ....

Algebra — Expanding Double Brackets

It's best to stick to this method — otherwise you're bound to miss one of the terms.

To multiply out double brackets use <u>FOIL</u>:	
<u>F</u>irst — Multiply the first terms in each bracket <u>O</u>utside — Multiply the outside terms <u>I</u>nside — Multiply the inside terms <u>L</u>ast — Multiply the last terms	Eg $(x + 2)(3x - 4)$ $= (x \times 3x) + (x \times -4) + (2 \times 3x) + (2 \times -4)$ $= 3x^2 - 4x + 6x - 8$ $= 3x^2 + 2x - 8$

Q1 For each of the large rectangles below,
write down the <u>area</u> of the four smaller rectangles.

a)

.... ' ....

.... ' ....

b)

.... ' ....

.... ' ....

c)

.... ' ....

.... ' ....

Q2 Multiply out the brackets and simplify your answers where possible:

a) $(x + 4)(x + 2)$

....

b) $(y + 8)(y + 5)$

....

c) $(z + 10)(z + 3)$

....

(Use your answers to **Q1** to help you check you've multiplied out the brackets correctly.)

Q3 Expand the brackets and simplify:

a) $(x + 1)(x + 2) =$

....

b) $(x + 3)(x + 2) =$

....

c) $(x + 4)(x + 5) =$

....

d) $(x + 5)(x - 1) =$

....

e) $(2x + 2)(x - 3) =$

....

f) $(x - 3)(3x + 1) =$

....

Algebra — Taking Out Common Factors

<u>**FACTORISING**</u> is just <u>putting the brackets back in</u>.
And when you've just spent all that time getting rid of them...

$$7x^2 + 21xy = 7x(x + 3y)$$

largest number that will go into 7 and 21	highest power of x, that will go into each term	y is not in every term so it is not a common factor, and goes inside the brackets

Q1   Factorise the expressions below. Each has <u>4</u> as a common factor.

   a) $4x + 8$ = ...

   c) $4 - 16x$ = ...

   b) $12 - 8x$ = ...

   d) $4x^2 + 64$ = ...

Q2   Factorise the expressions below. Each has <u>7</u> as a common factor.

   a) $21 - 7x$ = ...

   c) $14 + 21x$ = ...

   b) $28x + 7$ = ...

   d) $35x^2 - 14$ = ...

Q3   Factorise the expressions below. Each has <u>x</u> as a common factor.

   a) $2x + x^2$ = ...

   c) $x - 16x^2$ = ...

   b) $2x - x^2$ = ...

   d) $4x^2 - 3x$ = ...

Q4   Factorise the expressions below. Each has <u>2x</u> as a common factor.

   a) $2x + 4x^2$ = ...

   c) $2x - 16x^2$ = ...

   b) $2x - 8x^3$ = ...

   d) $4xy - 6x^2$ = ...

Q5   Factorise the expressions below by taking out any <u>common factors</u>.

   a) $2x + 4$ = ...

   f) $30 + 10x$ = ...

   b) $3x + 12$ = ...

   g) $9x^2 + 3x$ = ...

   c) $24 + 12x$ = ...

   h) $5x^2 + 10x$ = ...

   d) $16x + 4y$ = ...

   i) $7x^2 + 21x$ = ...

   e) $3x + 15$ = ...

   j) $3y + xy^2$ = ...

First look for any numbers the terms have in common, then look for the letters.

Special Number Sequences

There are five special sequences: EVEN, ODD, SQUARE, CUBE and TRIANGLE NUMBERS. You really need to know them and their nth terms.

Q1 What are these sequences called, and what are their next 3 terms?

a) 2, 4, 6, 8, …

....

b) 1, 3, 5, 7, …

....

c) 1, 4, 9, 16, …

....

d) 1, 8, 27, 64, …

....

e) 1, 3, 6, 10, …

....

Q2 The following sequences are described in words. Write down their first four terms.

a) The prime numbers starting from 37.

....

b) The powers of 2 starting from 32.

....

c) The squares of odd numbers starting from $7^2 = 49$.

....

d) The powers of 10 starting from 1000.

....

e) The triangular numbers starting from 15. The nth term is ½n(n + 1) — you're starting from n = 5.

....

UNIT TWO

Number Patterns

Q1   Draw the next two pictures in each pattern.
How many match sticks are used in each picture?

a)

,   ,

....

b)

Look for patterns in the numbers as well as pictures.

....

,

....

c)

,   ,   ,   ,

....

Q2   Look for the pattern and then fill in the next three lines. Some of the answers are too big to fit on a calculator display so you must spot the pattern.

a) 7×6 $= 42$

67×66 $= 4422$

667×666 $= 444222$

6667×6666 $= $ ....

66667×66666 $= $ ....

666667×666666 $= $ ....

b) $1 \times 81 = 81$

$21 \times 81 = 1701$

$321 \times 81 = 26001$

$4321 \times 81 = 350001$

$54321 \times 81 = $ ....

$654321 \times 81 = $ ....

$7654321 \times 81 = $ ....

UNIT TWO

Number Patterns

Q3 In each of the questions below, write down the next three numbers in the sequence and write the rule that you used.

> *Once you've worked out the next numbers, go back and write down exactly what you did — that will be the rule you're after.*

a) 1, 3, 5, 7, ... , ... , ... Rule ....

b) 2, 4, 8, 16, ... , ... , ... Rule ....

c) 3, 30, 300, 3000, ... , ... , ... Rule ....

d) 3, 7, 11, 15, ... , ... , ... Rule ....

e) 19, 14, 9, 4, –1, ... , ... , ... Rule ....

Q4 The letter n describes the position of a term in the sequence. For example, if $n = 1$, that's the 1st term…if $n = 10$ that's the 10th term and so on.
In the following, use the rule given to generate (or make) the first 5 terms.

a) $3n + 1$ so if $n = 1$ the 1st term is $\underline{(3 \times 1) + 1} = \underline{4}$

$n = 2$ the 2nd term is .... = ...

$n = 3$ .... = ...

$n = 4$ .... = ...

$n = 5$ .... = ...

b) $5n - 2$, when $n = 1, 2, 3, 4$ and 5
produces the sequence .... , ... , ... , ... , ...

c) n^2, when $n = 1, 2, 3, 4$, and 5
produces the sequence .... , ... , ... , ... , ...

d) $n^2 - 3$, when $n = 1, 2, 3, 4$, and 5
produces the sequence .... , ... , ... , ... , ...

Q5 Write down an expression for the nth term of the following sequences:

a) 2, 4, 6, 8, …

....

> *Remember the formula — $dn + (a - d)$.*

b) 1, 3, 5, 7, …

....

c) 5, 10, 15, 20, …

....

d) 5, 8, 11, 14, …

....

Metric and Imperial Units

You'd better learn ALL these conversions
— you'll be well and truly scuppered without them.

APPROXIMATE CONVERSIONS

1 kg = 2.2 lbs   1 gallon = 4.5 l   1 inch = 2.5 cm

1 litre = 1.75 pints   5 miles = 8 km

Q1 The table shows the distances in miles between 4 cities in Scotland. Fill in the blank table with the equivalent distances in kilometres.

Aberdeen			
105	Inverness		
150	175	Glasgow	
125	155	45	Edinburgh

Aberdeen			
	Inverness		
		Glasgow	
			Edinburgh

Q2 Change each of these weights from kilograms to pounds.

10 kg = ... lbs   16 kg = ... lbs   75 kg = ... lbs

Change each of these capacities in gallons to litres.

5 galls = ... l   14 galls = ... l   40 galls = ... l

Q3 Convert the measurements of the note book and pencil to centimetres.

12 in = ... cm

8 in = ... cm

5 in = ... cm

5 in

UNIT TWO

Conversion Factors

The method for these questions is very easy so you might as well learn it...

> 1) Find the <u>Conversion Factor</u>
> 2) <u>Multiply by it AND divide by it</u>
> 3) Choose the <u>common sense answer</u>

The conversion factor is the link between the two units — e.g. there are 100 cm in a m so the conversion factor is 100.

Q1   Fill in the gaps using the conversion factors:

20 mm = ... cm   82 mm = ... cm   .... mm = 6 cm

142 cm = ... m   .... cm = 2.5 m   2550 mm = ... m

9000 m = ... km   3470 m = ... km   .... m = 2 km

3 km = ... cm   .... mm = 3.4 m   .... cm = 0.5 km

6200 mg = ... g   8550 g = ... kg   2.3 kg = ... g

12 000 000 mg = ... kg   1.2 l = ... ml   4400 ml = ... l

Q2   Cashbags Bank are offering the following exchange rates:

> 18 Mexican Pesos to £1 Sterling.
> 200 Japanese Yen to £1 Sterling.
> 2 Canadian Dollars to £1 Sterling.

Use these exchange rates to calculate to the nearest penny the Sterling equivalent of:

a) 200 Mexican Pesos

....

b) 765 Japanese Yen

....

c) 73 Canadian Dollars

....

Using the same exchange rates, convert the following into Canadian Dollars:

d) £56

....

e) 1000 Japanese Yen

....

Q3   1 pint = 0.5714 litres. Which is better value,
2 pints of orange juice for £1.20 or 1 litre of orange juice for 95p?

Start by changing the 2 pints to litres.

....

Speed

This is an easy enough formula — and of course you can put it in that good old formula triangle as well.

Average speed = $\dfrac{\text{Total distance}}{\text{Total time}}$

Q1 A train travels 240 km in 4 hours. What is its <u>average speed</u>?

....

Q2 A car travels for 3 hours at an average speed of 55 mph. How far has it travelled?

....

Q3 <u>Complete</u> this table.

Distance Travelled	Time taken	Average Speed
210 km	3 hrs	
135 miles		30 mph
	2 hrs 30 mins	42 km/h
9 miles	45 mins	
640 km		800 km/h
	1 hr 10 mins	60 mph

Q4 An athlete can run 100 m in 11 seconds.
Calculate the athlete's speed in:

a) m/s

....

b) km/h

....

Q5 A plane flies over city A at 09.55 and over city B at 10.02.
What is its <u>average</u> speed if these cities are 63 miles apart?

....

Q6 The distance from Kendal (Oxenholme) to London (Euston) is 280 miles. The train travels at an average speed of 63 mph. If I catch the 07.05 from Kendal, can I be at a meeting in London by 10.30? <u>Show all your working</u>.

....

Density

Here we go again — the <u>multi-purpose formula triangle</u>. <u>Learn</u> the positions of <u>M, D and V</u>, plug in the <u>numbers</u> and pull out the <u>answer</u>... magic.

$$DENSITY = \frac{mass}{volume}$$

Q1 Find the <u>density</u> of each of these pieces of wood, giving your answer in g/cm³:

a) Mass 3 g, volume 4 cm³

....

b) Mass 20 g, volume 25 cm³

....

c) Mass 12 kg, volume 20,000 cm³

....

d) Mass 14 kg, volume 0.02 m³.

....

Q2 Calculate the <u>mass</u> of each of these objects:

a) a small marble statue of density
2.6 g/cm³ and volume 24 cm³   ....

b) a plastic cube of volume 64 cm³
and density 1.5 g/cm³   ....

c) a gold ingot with density 19.5 g/cm³
measuring 12 cm by 4 cm by 4 cm   ....

d) a pebble with volume 30 cm³
and density 2.5 g/cm³.   ....

Q3 Work out the <u>volume</u> of each of these items:

a) a bag of sugar of mass 1 kg and density 1.6 g/cm³

....

b) a packet of margarine with density 2.8 g/cm³ and mass 250 g

....

c) a 50 kg sack of coal with density 1.8 g/cm³

....

d) a box of cereal with density 0.2 g/cm³ and mass 500 g.

....

Quadrilaterals

Here's a few easy marks for you — all you've got to do is remember the shapes and a few facts about them... it's a waste of marks not to bother.

Fill in the blanks in the table.

NAME	DRAWING	DESCRIPTION
Square		Sides of equal length. Opposite sides parallel. Four right angles.
....	....	Opposite sides parallel and the same length. Four right angles.
....		Opposite sides are .... and Equal. Opposite angles are equal.
Trapezium		Only .... sides are parallel.
Rhombus		A parallelogram but with all sides ....
Kite	....	Two pairs of adjacent equal sides.

Families of Triangle

Q1 Fill in the gaps in these sentences.

a) An isosceles triangle has .... equal sides and .... equal angles.

b) A triangle with all its sides equal and all its angles equal is called an

.... triangle.

c) A scalene triangle has .... equal sides and .... equal angles.

d) A triangle with one right-angle is called a .... triangle.

Q2 By joining dots draw four different isosceles triangles, one in each box.

Q3 Using three different coloured pencils:
Find an equilateral triangle and shade it in.
Using a different colour, shade in two different
right angled triangles.
With your last colour shade in two different
scalene triangles.

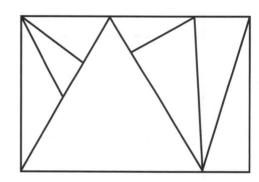

Q4 How many triangles are there in this diagram?

....

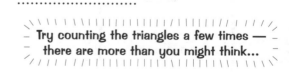

*Try counting the triangles a few times —
there are more than you might think...*

What sort of triangles are they?

....

There are only 4 types of triangles, so make sure you know them all
— think of all those nice fat juicy marks...

Perimeters

What you've gotta do with these is add up all the sides to get the perimeter.
If there's no drawing, do one yourself — then you won't forget any of the sides.

Q1   Work out the perimeters of the following shapes :

a)

Square Perimeter = ... cm

b)

Rectangle Perimeter =

= (2 × ......) + (2 × ......) = ... m

c)

Equilateral Triangle

Perimeter = 3 × ...... = ... cm

d)

Triangle

Perimeter = ... + ... + ...

= .... cm

e)

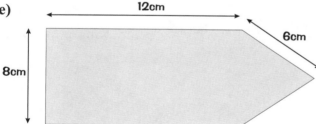

Symmetrical Five Sided Shape

Perimeter = ... + ... + ... + ... + ...

= .... cm

f)

Symmetrical Four Sided Shape

Perimeter = ... + ... + ... + ... = ... cm

Q2 a) A square garden has sides of length 10 m.
How much fencing is needed to go around it?   .... m.

b) A photo measures 17.5 cm by 12.5 cm.
What is the total length of the frame around it?   .... cm.

UNIT TWO

Perimeters

Q3 Find the perimeter of these shapes (you may need to work out some of the lengths):

a)

Perimeter ....

b)

Perimeter ....

c)

Perimeter ....

d)

Perimeter ....

e)

Perimeter ....

f)

Perimeter ....

Areas of Rectangles

For rectangles and squares, working out the area is a piece of pie — it's just **LENGTH TIMES WIDTH**. Nowt more to it.

AREA = LENGTH × WIDTH

Q1   Calculate the areas of the following rectangles:

a) Length = 10 cm, Width = 4 cm,   Area = ... × ..... = ... cm².

b) Length = 55 cm, Width = 19 cm, Area = ... cm².

c) Length = 12 m,   Width = 7 m,   Area = ... m².

d) Length = 155 m, Width = 28 m,   Area = ... m².

e) Length = 3.7 km, Width = 1.5 km, Area = ... km².

Q2   Measure the lengths and widths of each of these rectangles, then calculate the area.

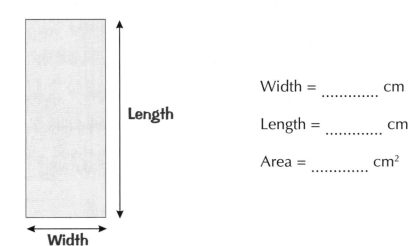

a)

Width = ... cm

Length = ... cm

Area = ... cm²

b)

Width = ... cm

Length = ... cm

Area = ... cm²

Areas of Triangles

Triangles aren't much different, but <u>remember</u> to **TIMES BY THE ½.**

Area = ½ (Base × Height)

Q1   Calculate the areas of the following triangles:

a) Base = 12 cm, Height = 9 cm,   Area = $\frac{1}{2}$ (........ × ....) = ... cm².

b) Base = 5 cm, Height = 3 cm,   Area = ... cm².

c) Base = 25 m, Height = 7 m,   Area = ... m².

d) Base = 1.6 m, Height = 6.4 m,   Area = ... m².

e) Base = 700 cm, Height = 350 cm,   Area = ... cm².

Q2   Measure the base and height of each of these triangles, then calculate the area.

a)

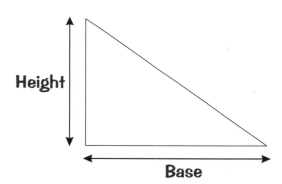

Height = ... cm

Base = ... cm

Area = ... cm²

b)

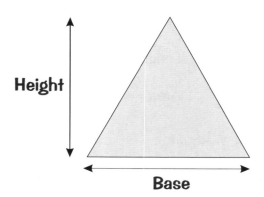

Height = ... cm

Base = ... cm

Area = ... cm²

Composite Areas

Bit more tricky, these... but look — they're all just rectangles and triangles.
Work out each bit separately, then add the areas together — easy.

Calculate the areas of these composite shapes...

Q1

Shape A: length = ... width = ...

Area = ... × .... = ... cm²

Shape B: length = ... width = ...

Area = ... × .... = ... cm²

Total (area A + area B) = ... + ... = ... cm²

Q2

Shape A (rectangle): .... × .... = ... cm²

Shape B (triangle): ½ (base x height)

Base = ... cm , Height = ... cm

Area = ½ (........ × ....) = ... cm²

Total Area = ... + ... = ... cm²

Q3

Shape A (rectangle): .... × .... = ... cm²

Shape B (triangle): ½ (........ × ....) = ... cm²

Total Area = ... + ... = ... cm²

Q4 Draw a dotted line to divide this shape.

Shape A (rectangle): .... × .... = ... cm²

Shape B (triangle): ½(........ × ....) = ... cm²

Total Area = ... + ... = ... cm²

Q5

Draw dotted lines to divide this shape.

Shape A (rectangle): .... × .... = ... cm²

Shape B (square): .... × .... = ... cm²

Total Area = (4 × Shape A) + Shape B = ... cm²

Solids and Nets

Q1 Which of the following nets would make a cube? ....

a)

b)

c)

d)

e)

f)

Q2 On a separate piece of paper, draw an accurate net for each of the following solids.

a)

b)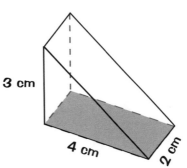

Q3 This net will make a common, mathematical solid. Name the solid:

....

 You've got to think about folding the net up to make the shape —
if you're struggling, the best thing to do is practise your origami skills...

Volume

Q1 Each shape has been made from centimetre cubes. The volume of a centimetre cube is 1 cubic cm. How many cubes are there in each shape? What is the volume of each shape?

a)

There are ..12.. cubes.
The volume is
..12.. cubic cm.

b)

There are ...... cubes.
The volume is
...... cubic cm.

c)

There are ...... cubes.
The volume is
...... cubic cm.

d)

There are ...... cubes.
The volume is
...... cubic cm.

e)

There are ...... cubes.
The volume is
...... cubic cm.

f)

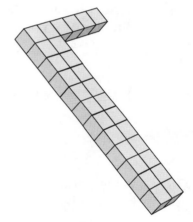

There are ...... cubes.
The volume is
...... cubic cm.

g)

There are ...... cubes.
The volume is ...... cubic cm.

h)

There are ...... cubes.
The volume is ...... cubic cm.

You simply add up the cubes... but make sure you don't miss any
— remember that there are some rows at the back too.

Unit Two

Volume

Finding volumes of cubes and cuboids is just like finding areas of squares and rectangles — except you've got an extra side to multiply by.

Q2   A match box measures 7 cm by 4 cm by 5 cm. What is its volume?

   ....

Q3   A cereal box measures 30 cm by 6 cm by 15 cm. What is its volume?

   ....

Q4   A video cassette case measures 20 cm by 3 cm by 10 cm. What is its volume?

   ....

Q5   A room is 2.5 m tall, 8 m long and 5 m wide. What is its volume?

   ....

Q6   Which holds more, a box measuring 12 cm by 5 cm by 8 cm or a box measuring 10 cm by 6 cm by 9 cm?

   ....

Q7   What is the volume of a cube of side:

   a) 5 cm? ....

   b) 9 cm? ....

   c) 15 cm? ....

Q8   A box measures 9 cm by 5 cm by 8 cm. What is its volume? ....
   What is the volume of a box twice as long,
   twice as wide and twice as tall?   ....

Q9   An ice cube measures 2 cm by 2 cm by 2 cm. What is its volume? ....
   Is there enough room in a container measuring
   8 cm by 12 cm by 10 cm for 100 ice cubes?

   ....

Estimating Angles

**Estimating angles is easy once you know the 4 special angles —
you can use them as reference points.**

For each of the angles below write down its type, estimate its size (before you
measure it!) and finally measure each angle with a protractor. The first one has
been done for you.

Angle	Type	Estimated Size	Actual Size
a	acute	40°	43°
b			
c			
d			
e			
f			

Drawing Angles

These instruments are used to measure angles.

An angle measurer.

A protractor.

Don't forget protractors have two scales — one going one way and one the other... so make sure you measure from the one that starts with 0°, not 180°.

Q1   Use an angle measurer or protractor to help you to draw the following angles.

a)   20°   b)   65°   c)   90°

d)   136°   e)   225°   f)   340°

Q2 a) Draw an acute angle and measure it.   **b)** Draw an obtuse angle and measure it.

Acute angle measures .... °   Obtuse angle measures .... °

c) Draw a reflex angle and measure it.

Reflex angle measures .... °

Compass Directions

Q1

Start at the dot in the middle of the bottom line
and follow the directions. What shape have you drawn? ....

a) West 4 squares.
b) North 4 squares.
c) East 4 squares.
d) South 4 squares.
e) North East through 2 squares.

f) North 4 squares.
g) South West through 2 squares.
h) West 4 squares.
i) North East through 2 squares.
j) East 4 squares.

Q2

N

Joe's house

Shop

Church

Sue's house

Park

Jane's house

a) What direction does Jane go to get to Sue's house? ....

b) What direction is the church from Joe's house? ....

c) What is South East of Sue's house? ....

d) What is West of Sue's house? ....

e) Jane is at home. She is going to meet Sue in the park. They are going to the shop and
then to Joe's house. Write down Jane's directions.

....

You could use "__Never Eat Shredded Wheat__" but it's more fun to make one up
— like __Not Everyone Squeezes Wombats__, or __Nine Elves Storm Wales__... (hmm)

UNIT TWO

Three Figure Bearings

Bearings always have three digits — even the small ones...
in other words, if you've measured 60°, you've got to write it as 060°.

This is a map of part of a coastline. The scale is one cm to one km.

Q1 What is the bearing of the 🚐 from the ⓘ? ....

Q2 What is the bearing of the 🅿 from the 🏊? ....

Q3 How far and on what bearing is...

a) The boat from the plane? ....

b) The boat from the oil rig? ....

c) The plane from the oil rig? ....

Q4 The water ski centre is on a bearing of 050° from the golf course, and at a distance of 4.5 km. Put a ☆ where the ski centre is.

Do the direction bit first — and draw a straight line. Then measure the correct distance along it.

Q5 There is a lighthouse on the coast. It is at a bearing of 300° from the oil rig and a bearing of 270° from the boat. Mark its position with a △.

Angle Rules

Hope you've learnt those angle rules for a straight line and round a point...

Q1 Work out the angles labelled:

a = ...

120°   a

b = ...

76°   b

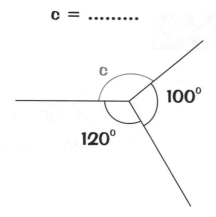

c = ...

c

100°

120°

d = ...

87°   d

118°   125°

e = ...

f = ...

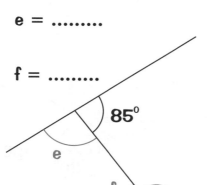

85°

e

f   138°

g = ...

h = ...

i = ...

g

41°

h   53°

i

Angle Rules

Q2

> ### The three angles inside a triangle always add up to 180°

Work out the missing angle in each of these triangles. The angles are not drawn to scale so you cannot measure them.

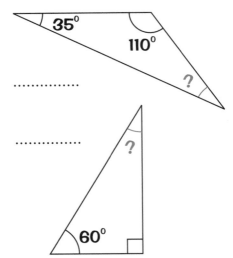

> ### The angles in a quadrilateral always add up to 360°

Q3   Work out the missing angles in these quadrilaterals.

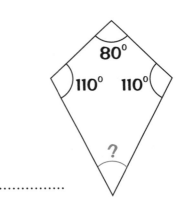

Q4   Work out the missing angles in these diagrams.

a = ...

b = ...

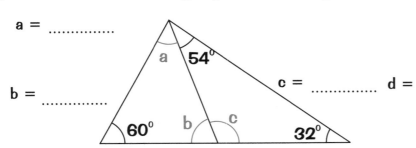

c = ...   d = ...

e = ...

You'd better get learning these rules too — they're not that hard,
and you'll be well and truly stumped without them.

Parallel Lines

Once you know the 3 ANGLE RULES for parallel lines, you can find all the angles out from just one — ah, such fun...

c = f and d = e — Alternate angles

a = e, c = g, b = f and d = h — Corresponding angles

$d + f = 180^0$, $c + e = 180^0$ — Supplementary angles

Find the sizes of the angles marked by letters in these diagrams. Write down what sort of angle each one is.

NOT DRAWN TO SCALE

a = ...

b = ...

c = ...

d = ...

e = ...

f = ...

g = ...

h = ...

i = ...

j = ...

UNIT TWO

Midpoints of Line Segments

Q1   Find the midpoint of the line segments AB, where A and B have coordinates:

a) A(2,3)   B(4,5)   ....

d) A(3,15)   B(13,3)   ....

b) A(1,8)   B(9,2)   ....

e) A(6,6)   B(0,0)   ....

c) A(0,11)   B(12,11)   ....

f) A(15,9)   B(3,3)   ....

Your answers should be coordinates too.

ahh... nice'n'easy...

Q2   Find the midpoints of each of these line segments:

a) Line segment PQ, where P has coordinates (1,5) and Q has coordinates (5,6).

....

b) Line segment AB, where A has coordinates (3,3) and B has coordinates (4,0).

....

c) Line segment RS, where R has coordinates (4,5) and S has coordinates (0,0).

....

d) Line segment PQ, where P has coordinates (1,3) and Q has coordinates (3,1).

....

e) Line segment GH, where G has coordinates (0,0) and H has coordinates (–6,–7).

....

Q3   Find the midpoint of each of the line segments on this graph.

AB: ....

CD: ....

EF: ....

GH: ....

JK: ....

LM: ....

Coordinates

Q1 On the grid plot the following points. Label the points A,B…
Join the points with straight lines as you plot them.

A(0,8) B(4,6) C(4.5,6.5) D(5,6) E(9,8) F(8,5.5) G(5,5) H(8,4) I(7.5,2) J(6,2) K(5,4) L(4.5,3.5) M(4,4) N(3,2) O(1.5,2) P(1,4) Q(4,5) R(1,5.5) S(0,8).

You should see the outline of an insect. What is it? ....

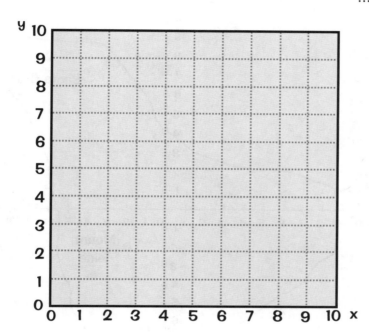

You've got to get your coordinates in the right order — or they're totally useless — you always go IN THE HOUSE then UP THE STAIRS.

Q2 Write down the letter which is by each of the following points.
The sentence it spells is the answer to question one.

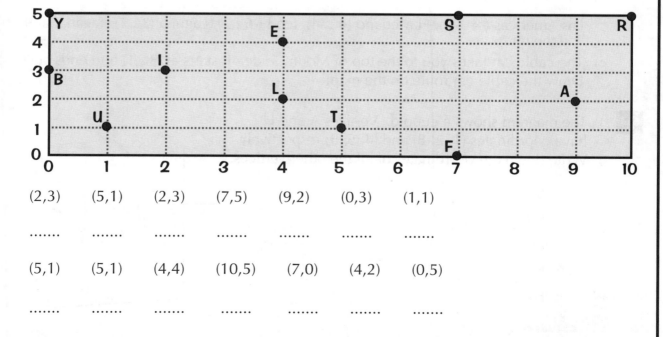

(2,3)	(5,1)	(2,3)	(7,5)	(9,2)	(0,3)	(1,1)
....	....	....	....	....	....	....

(5,1)	(5,1)	(4,4)	(10,5)	(7,0)	(4,2)	(0,5)
....	....	....	....	....	....	....

72

Coordinates

Remember — 1) **X comes before Y**

2) **X goes a-cross (get it) the page.** (Ah, the old ones are the best...)

Q3 The map shows the island of Tenerife where the sun never stops shining...

a) Use the map to write down the coordinates of the following:

Airport (.... , ...)

Mount Teide (.... , ...)

Santa Cruz (.... , ...)

Puerto Colon (.... , ...)

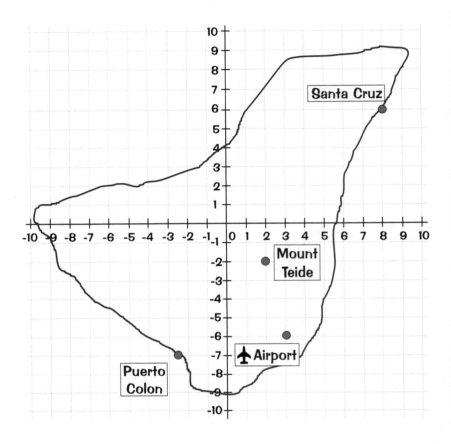

b) Use the coordinates given to mark the following holiday destinations on the map.

Las Americas (-4 , -6), El Medano (4 , -4), Icod (-6 , 2), Laguna (3 , 7), Taganana (9 , 9)

c) The cable car takes you to the top of Mount Teide. It starts at (3 , 1) and ends at (2 , -2). Draw the cable car route on the map.

Q4 The diagram shows a cuboid. Vertices A and H have coordinates (1, 2, 8) and (4, 5, 3) respectively. Write down the coordinates of all the other vertices.

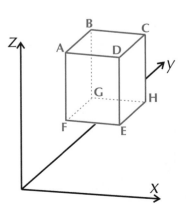

B (.... , ... , ...)

C (.... , ... , ...)

D (.... , ... , ...)

E (.... , ... , ...)

F (.... , ... , ...)

G (.... , ... , ...)

UNIT TWO

Straight Line Graphs

The <u>very first thing</u> you've got to do is work out a <u>table of values</u>.

Example: Draw the graph of y = 3x − 1 for values of x between 0 and 4.

1) First complete a <u>table of values</u>:

x	0	1	2	3	4
y	-1	2	5	8	11

← decided by the question

← worked out using y = 3x - 1

2) Draw the axes.
3) Plot the points.
4) Draw a straight line through the points.

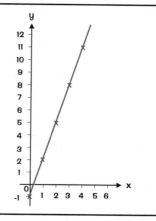

Q1 On the grid shown, draw axes with x from 0 to 8 and y from 0 to 14.

Q2 a) Complete the table of values, for y = x + 2.

x	0	1	2	3	4	5	6
y	2			5			

b) Use your <u>table of values</u> to draw the graph of y = x + 2 on the grid opposite.

Q3 a) Complete the table below, for y = 2x + 1

x	0	1	2	3	4	5	6
y	1				9		

b) Use your <u>table of values</u> to draw the graph y = 2x + 1 on the grid opposite.

Q4 a) Fill in the table for y = 8 − x, using values of x from 0 to 6.

x	0	1	2	3	4	5	6
y							

b) Draw the graph of y = 8 − x.

Straight Line Graphs

The equations of most straight line graphs can be written in the form:

$$y = mx + c$$

The number multiplying the x term tells you the **gradient** of the graph

The number by itself tells you where the graph crosses the y axis. This is the **y-intercept**

Q5 On the grid to the right, draw the lines:

$y = 2$, $x = 5$, $y = 4$, $x = 0$, $y = -1$, $x = -2$.

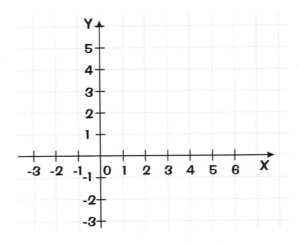

Q6 The following are equations of linear graphs. <u>Without plotting</u> the graphs, state the <u>gradient</u> of each graph and the <u>y-intercept</u>.

a) $y = 4x + 2$ ....

b) $y = 5x - 1$ ....

c) $y = 6x$ ....

d) $y = 5 + 2x$ ....

e) $y = 12 - 3x$ ....

f) $y = x$ ....

g) $y = 3 - x$ ....

h) $y + 2x = 10$ ....

i) $2y = x + 4$ ....

j) $y + 5 = 4x$ ....

Q7 Find the values for m and c if the linear graph $y = mx + c$ has a gradient of 3 and passes through (0, 8).

....

Q8 Find the values for m and c if the linear graph $y = mx + c$ has a gradient of 1 and passes through (2, 0).

....

Ratio

I think I can spot another Golden Rule lurking here...
DIVIDE FOR ONE, THEN TIMES FOR ALL.

Q1 To make grey paint, black and white paint are mixed in the ratio 5:3. How much black paint would be needed with:

a) 6 litres of white? ....

b) 12 litres of white? ....

c) 21 litres of white? ....

Q2 To make orange squash you mix water and concentrated orange juice in the ratio 9:2. How much water is needed with:

a) 10 ml of concentrated juice? ....

b) 30 ml of concentrated juice? ....

c) 42 ml of concentrated juice? ....

Q3 The ratio of men to women at a football match was 11:4.
How many men were there if there were:

a) 2000 women? ....

b) 8460 women? ....

How many women were there if there were:

c) 22000 men? ....

d) 6820 men? ....

Ratio

Q4   Divide the following quantities in the given ratio.

For example:

£400 in the ratio 1 : 4   1 + 4 = 5   400 ÷ 5 = 80

<u>1 × £80 = £80 and 4 × 80 = £320</u>   <u>£80 : £320</u>

a) 100 g in the ratio 1 : 4   .... + ... = ... ÷ .... = ...

.... × .... = ... and .... × ...... = ...

= ...... : ......

b) 500 m in the ratio 2 : 3 = ... : ....

c) £12000 in the ratio 1 : 2 = ... : ....

d) 6.3 kg in the ratio 3 : 4 = ... : ....

e) £8.10 in the ratio 4 : 5 = ... : ....

Q5   Now try these…

a) Adam and Mags win £24 000. They split the money in the ratio 1 : 5. How much does Adam get?

....

b) Sunil and Paul compete in a pizza eating contest. Between them they consume 28 pizzas in the ratio 3 : 4. Who wins and how many did they eat?

.... eats .... pizzas

c) The total distance covered in a triathlon (swimming, cycling and running) is 15km. It is split in the ratio 2 : 3 : 5. How far is each section?

Swimming = ..., cycling = ..., running = ...

A great way to check your answer works is to add up the individual quantities — they should add up to the original amount.

Best Buys

Start by finding the AMOUNT PER PENNY — the more
of the stuff you get per penny, the better value it is.

Q1

The small bar of chocolate weighs 50 g and costs 32p.
The large bar weighs 200 g and costs 80p.

a) How many grams do you get for 1p from the small bar?

....

b) How many grams do you get for 1p from the large bar?

....

c) Which bar gives you more for your money?

....

Q2   The large tin of tuna weighs 400 g and costs £1.05.
The small tin weighs 220 g and costs 57p.

a) How many grams do you get for 1p in the large tin?

....

b) How many grams do you get for 1p in the small tin?

....

c) Which tin gives better value for money?

....

Q3   Which of these boxes of eggs is better value for money?

....

60p   £1.10   ....

Fractions of Quantities

Q1 Write down the following quantities…

a) Half of 12 = ……..

b) Quarter of 24 = ……..

c) Third of 30 = ……..

d) 1/4 of 44 = ……..

e) 3/4 of 60 = ……..

f) 2/3 of 6 = ……..

Q2 Calculate the fractions of the following …

eg. 1/3 of 18 = 18 ÷ 3 = <u>6</u>

a) 1/8 of 32 = …….. ÷ 8 = ……..

b) 1/10 of 50 = …….. ÷ 10 = ……..

c) 1/12 of 144 = …….. ÷ …….. = ……..

d) 1/25 of 75 = …….. ÷ …….. = ……..

e) 1/30 of 180 = …….. ÷ …….. = ……..

f) 1/27 of 540 = …….. ÷ …….. = ……..

Q3 Calculate the fractions of the following…

eg. 2/5 of 50   50 ÷ 5 = 10   2 × 10 = <u>20</u>

a) 2/3 of 60   60 ÷ 3 = ……..   2 × …….. = ……..

b) 4/5 of 25   25 ÷ …….. = ……..   4 × …….. = ……..

c) 7/9 of 63   …….. ÷ …….. = ……..   …….. × …….. = ……..

d) 3/10 of 100   …….. ÷ …….. = ……..   …….. × …….. = ……..

e) 12/19 of 760   …….. ÷ …….. = ……..   …….. × …….. = ……..

f) 6/9 of £1.80   …….. ÷ …….. = ……..   …….. × …….. = £…….. or …….. p

g) 10/18 of £9.00   …….. ÷ …….. = ……..   …….. × …….. = £……..

h) 2/3 of one day (24 hours)   …….. ÷ …….. = ……..   …….. × …….. = …….. hours

i) 5/6 of one year (12 months)   …….. ÷ …….. = ……..   …….. × …….. = …….. months

j) 2/5 of one kilogram (1000 grams)   ……………………… = ……….. g

DIVIDE BY THE BOTTOM, TIMES BY THE TOP
— and suddenly fractions don't seem so bad…

Fraction Arithmetic

Fraction arithmetic becomes a nice cruise in the park, once you've learned the rules for dealing with each type of sum.

> **MULTIPLYING:** just multiply the <u>tops</u> and the <u>bottoms</u>.
> **DIVIDING:** turn the second fraction <u>upside down</u>, then <u>multiply them</u>.
> **ADDING OR SUBTRACTING:**
> 1) Make the bottom number <u>the same</u> (get "a common denominator")
> 2) Add or subtract the top numbers <u>only</u>.

Answer the following questions <u>without</u> using a calculator.

Q1 Change these top-heavy fractions to mixed numbers:

For some of the questions below, you'll need to change the mixed fractions into top-heavy fractions at the start.

a) $\frac{3}{2} =$ ....   b) $\frac{7}{4} =$ ....   c) $\frac{8}{3} =$ ....

Change these mixed numbers to top-heavy fractions:

d) $2\frac{1}{2} =$ ....   e) $3\frac{1}{3} =$ ....   f) $1\frac{3}{5} =$ ....

Q2 Do the following multiplications, expressing the answers as fractions in their lowest terms:

a) $\frac{4}{3} \times \frac{3}{4}$ ....   d) $2\frac{1}{2} \times \frac{3}{5}$ ....

b) $\frac{2}{5} \times \frac{3}{4}$ ....   e) $10\frac{2}{7} \times \frac{7}{9}$ ....

c) $\frac{11}{9} \times \frac{6}{5}$ ....   f) $2\frac{1}{6} \times 3\frac{1}{3}$ ....

Q3 Carry out the following divisions, and express each answer in its lowest terms:

a) $\frac{1}{4} \div \frac{3}{8}$ ....   d) $1\frac{1}{2} \div \frac{5}{12}$ ....

b) $\frac{1}{9} \div \frac{2}{3}$ ....   e) $10\frac{4}{5} \div \frac{9}{10}$ ....

c) $\frac{15}{24} \div \frac{6}{5}$ ....   f) $3\frac{7}{11} \div 1\frac{4}{11}$ ....

Q4 Add the two fractions, giving your answer as a fraction in its lowest terms:

a) $\frac{7}{8} + \frac{3}{8}$ ....   b) $\frac{1}{12} + \frac{3}{4}$ ....   c) $\frac{1}{3} + \frac{3}{4}$ ....

d) $1\frac{2}{5} + 2\frac{2}{3}$ ....   e) $\frac{1}{6} + 4\frac{1}{3}$ ....   f) $1\frac{3}{10} + \frac{2}{5}$ ....

Q5 Evaluate, giving your answer as a fraction in its lowest terms:

a) $\frac{11}{4} - \frac{2}{3}$ ....   b) $10 - \frac{2}{5}$ ....   c) $1\frac{3}{4} - 1\frac{1}{5}$ ....

d) $4\frac{2}{3} - \frac{7}{9}$ ....   e) $3\frac{1}{2} - \frac{2}{3}$ ....   f) $8 - \frac{1}{8}$ ....

More Fraction Problems

Try these questions without a calculator:

Q1   What fraction of 1 hour is:

a) 5 minutes ....

b) 15 minutes ....

c) 40 minutes? ....

Q2   If a TV programme lasts 40 minutes, what fraction of the programme is left after:

a) 10 minutes ....

b) 15 minutes ....

c) 35 minutes? ....

no calculators!!

Q3   In the fast food café, over all the shifts there are eighteen girls and twelve boys waiting at tables. In the kitchen there are six boys and nine girls. What fraction of the <u>kitchen staff</u> are girls, and what fraction of the <u>employees</u> are boys?

Fraction of kitchen staff who are girls ....

Fraction of employees who are boys ....

Use a calculator for the questions below.

Q4   At a college, two fifths of students are female, and three sevenths of these are part-time. If there are 2100 students altogether, how many:

a) are <u>female</u> students? ....

b) are <u>part-time</u> female students? ....

Q5   If I pay my gas bill within seven days, I get a <u>reduction</u> of an eighth of the price. If my bill is £120, how much can I save? ....

Q6   The wage bill at an office is £2400 in total. Fred gets one sixth, Greg gets a fifth of the remainder and Hilary gets what is left. How much money are each of them paid?

Fred ....,   Greg ....,   Hilary ....

Q7   In the summer three friends ran a car-cleaning service. They divided up the profits at the end of the summer according to the <u>proportion of cars</u> each had cleaned. Ali had washed 200 cars, Brenda had washed 50 and Chay had washed 175. The profits were £1700. How much did each person get?

Ali ....,   Brenda ....,   Chay ....

This is just like Q6, except you've got to work out the fractions of the money they get yourself.

Don't get put off by all the padding in the questions — you've just got to pick out the important stuff.

Percentages

Finding "something %" of "something-else" is really
quite simple — so you'd better be sure you know how.

| 1) "OF" means "×". | Example: 30% of 150 would be |
| 2) "PER CENT" means "OUT OF 100". | translated as $\dfrac{30}{100} \times 150 = 45$. |

Q1 Try these <u>without</u> a calculator:

a) 50% of £12 = ...

b) 25% of £20 = ...

c) 10% of £50 = ...

d) 5% of £50 = ...

e) 30% of £50 = ...

f) 75% of £80 = ...

g) 10% of 90 cm = ...

h) 10% of 4.39 kg = ...

Now you can use a calculator:

i) 8% of £16 = ...

j) 85% of 740 kg = ...

k) 40% of 40 minutes = ...

A school has 750 pupils.

l) If 56% of the pupils are boys, what percentage are girls? ....

m) How many boys are there in the school? ....

n) One day, 6% of the pupils were absent. How many pupils was this? ....

o) 54% of the pupils have a school lunch, 38% bring sandwiches and the rest go home for lunch. How many pupils go home for lunch?

....

Q2 VAT (value added tax) is charged at a rate of 17.5% on many goods and services. Complete the table showing how much VAT has to be paid and the new price of each article.

Article	Basic price	VAT at 17.5%	Price + VAT
Tin of paint	£6.75		
Paint brush	£3.60		
Sand paper	£1.55		

Percentages

Q3   John bought a new PC. The tag in the shop said it cost <u>£890+VAT</u>.
If VAT is charged at 17½%, how much did he pay?

....

Q4   Admission to Wonder World is <u>£18 for adults</u>. A child ticket is <u>60%</u> of the adult price.

a) How much will it cost for one adult and 4 children to enter Wonder World?

....

b) How much will two adults and three children spend on entrance tickets?

....

Q5   Daphne earns an annual wage of £18900. She doesn't pay tax on the first £3400 that
she earns. How much income tax does she pay when the rate of tax is:

a) 25% ? ....   **b)** 40% ? ....

Q6   Terence paid £4700 for his new motorcycle. <u>Each year</u> its value decreased by 12%.

a) How much was it worth when it was one year old? ....

b) How much was it worth when it was two years old? ....

Q7   A double-glazing salesman is paid 10% commission on every sale he makes.
In addition he is paid a £50 bonus if the sale is over £500.

a) If a customer buys £499 worth from the salesman,
what is his <u>commission</u>?

....

b) How much extra will he earn if he persuades the
customer in **a)** to spend an extra £20?

....

c) How much does he earn if he sells £820 worth of
windows?

....

Q8 | Bed & breakfast £37 per person.   Evening meal £15 per person |

THE
PICKLED
PARROT

2 people stay at The Pickled Parrot for 2 nights and have an evening meal
each night. How much is the total cost, if VAT is added at 17½% ?

....

More Standard Index Form

This stuff gets a lot easier if you know how to handle your calculator — read and learn.

Standard Index Form with a Calculator

Use the **EXP** button (or **EE** button) to enter numbers in standard index form.

Eg $1.7 \times 10^9 + 2.6 \times 10^{10}$ **1** **.** **7** **EXP** **9** **+** **2** **.** **6** **EXP** **10** **=**

The answer is $\boxed{2.77^{10}}$ which is read as 2.77×10^{10}

Q1 What is 7 million in standard index form? ....

Q2 Which is greater, 4.62×10^{12} or 1.04×10^{13}, and by how much? ....

Q3 Which is smaller 3.2×10^{-8} or 1.3×10^{-9} and by how much? ....

Q4 The following numbers are not written in standard index form.
Rewrite them correctly using standard index form.

a) 42×10^6 ....

b) 38×10^{-5} ....

c) 10×10^6 ....

d) 11.2×10^{-5} ....

e) 843×10^3 ....

f) 42.32×10^{-4} ....

Q5 One atomic mass unit is equivalent to 1.661×10^{-27} kg. What are two atomic mass units equivalent to (in standard index form)? ....

Q6 The radius of the Earth is 6.38×10^3 km. What is the radius of the Earth measured in cm? Leave your answer in standard form. ....

Q7 The length of a light year, the distance light can travel in one year, is 9.461×10^{15} m. Write in standard form the distance that light can travel in:

a) 2 years ....

b) 6 months ....

Q8 If $x = 4 \times 10^5$ and $y = 6 \times 10^4$ work out the value (in standard index form) of

a) xy ....

b) 4x ....

c) 3y ....

Don't forget — when you're using a calculator, you've got to write the answer as 3.46×10^{27}, not as 3.46^{27}. If you do it the wrong way, it means something completely different.

Formulas from Words

It's no big mystery — algebra is just like normal sums, but with the odd letter or two stuck in for good measure.

Q1 Write the algebraic expression for these:

a) Three more than x ....

d) y multiplied by y ....

b) Seven less than y ....

e) Ten divided by b ....

c) Four multiplied by x ....

f) A number add five ....

Q2 Steven is 16 years old. How old will he be in:

a) 5 years? ....

b) 10 years? ....

c) x years? ....

Q3 Tickets for a football match cost £25 each. What is the cost for:

a) 2 tickets? ....

b) 6 tickets? ....

c) y tickets? ....

CGP Wanderers Football Club

Vs United Rovers FC

Comfy Seat
East stand lower bit
Row 20
Seat 104

£25.00

Q4 There are n books in a pile. Write an expression for the number of books in a pile that has:

a) 3 more books ....

b) 4 fewer books ....

c) Twice as many books ....

Q5 a) I have 6 CDs and I buy 5 more. How many CDs have I now? ....

b) I have 6 CDs and I buy *w* more. How many CDs have I now? ....

c) I have x CDs and I buy *w* more. How many CDs have I now? ....

Q6 a) This square has sides of length 3 cm.

What is its perimeter? ....

What is its area? ....

b) This square has sides of length d cm.

What is its perimeter? ....

What is its area? ....

3 cm

3 cm

d cm

d cm

Substituting Values into Formulas

BODMAS — this funny little word helps you remember in which order to work formulas out. The example below shows you how to use it. Oh and by the way "**O**ther" might not seem important, but it means things like powers and square roots, etc — so it is.

Example: if $z = \frac{x}{10} + (y-3)^2$, find the value of z when x = 40 and y = 13.

1) Write down the formula with the numbers stuck in, $z = \frac{40}{10} + (13-3)^2$

2) <u>B</u>rackets first: $\qquad z = \frac{40}{10} + (10)^2$

3) <u>O</u>ther next, so square: $\qquad z = \frac{40}{10} + 100$

4) <u>D</u>ivision before <u>A</u>ddition: $\quad z = 4 + 100$
$$z = 104$$

Q1 If x = 3 and y = 6 find the value of the following expressions.

a) x + 2y ....
c) 4(x + y) ....
e) $2x^2$ ....

b) 2x ÷ y ....
d) $(y-x)^2$ ....
f) $2y^2$ ....

Q2 If V = lwh, find V when, **a)** l = 7, w = 5, h = 2 ....

b) l = 12, w = 8, h = 5. ....

Q3 Using the formula $z = (x-10)^2$, find the value of z when,

a) x = 20 ....
b) x = 15 ....
c) x = -1 ....

Q4 If V = u + at, find the <u>value of V</u> when u = 8, a = 9.8 and t = 2. ....

Q5 The cost, C pence, of hiring a taxi depends on the number, n, of miles you travel in it, where C = 100 + 25n. Find C when

a) n = 2 ....
b) n = 10 ....
c) n = 15 ....

Q6 The cost of framing a picture, C pence, depends on the <u>dimensions of the picture</u>. If C = 10L + 5W, where L is the length in cm and W is the width in cm, then find the cost of framing:

a) a picture of length 40 cm and width 24 cm ....

b) a square picture of sides 30 cm. ....

Q7 The time taken to cook a chicken is given as 20 minutes per lb plus 20 minutes extra. Find the time needed to cook a chicken weighing:

a) 4 lb ....

b) 7.5 lb ....

You need to write your own formula for this one.

Solving Equations

You've got to get the letter on its own (x = ...).
You can add, divide... well, anything really — but you gotta
do it to both sides or it'll all go horribly wrong.

Q1   Solve these equations:

a) a + 6 = 20

b) b + 12 = 30

c) 48 + c = 77

....

....

....

d) 397 + d = 842

e) e + 9.8 = 14.1

f) 3 + f = 7

....

....

....

Q2   Solve these equations:

a) g − 7 = 4

b) h − 14 = 11

c) i − 38 = 46

....

....

....

d) j − 647 = 353

e) k − 6.4 = 2.9

f) l − 7 = -4

....

....

....

Q3   Solve these equations:

a) 4m = 28

b) 7n = 84

c) 15p = 645

....

....

....

d) 279q = 1395

e) 6.4r = 9.6

f) -5s = 35

....

....

....

Q4   Solve these equations:

a) $\frac{t}{3} = 5$

b) u ÷ 6 = 9

c) $\frac{v}{11} = 8$

....

....

....

d) $\frac{w}{197} = 7$

e) x ÷ 1.8 = 7.2

f) $\frac{y}{-3} = 7$

....

....

....

Solving Equations

These are just like the last page... only there's an extra step.
It's a good idea to get rid of any fractions before you do anything else.

Q5   Solve these equations:

a) $3x + 2 = 14$

....

b) $5x - 4 = 31$

....

c) $8 + 6x = 50$

....

d) $20 - 3x = -61$

....

Q6   Solve these equations:

a) $\dfrac{x}{3} + 4 = 10$

....

b) $\dfrac{x}{5} - 9 = 6$

....

c) $4 + \dfrac{x}{9} = 6$

....

d) $\dfrac{x}{17} - 11 = 31$

....

For help with these, look back over <u>expanding brackets</u> and <u>collecting like terms</u>.

Q7   Solve these equations:

a) $3(2x + 1) = 27$

....

b) $2(4x + 1) + x = 56$

....

c) $5x + 3 = 2x + 15$

....

d) $2(x + 7) = 6x - 10$

....

Q8   Solve the following:

a) $3(7 - 2x) = 2(5 - 4x)$

....

b) $4(3x + 2) + 3 = 3(2x - 5) + 2$

....

c) $6(x + 2) + 4(x - 3) = 50$

....

d) $10(x + 3) - 4(x - 2) = 7(x + 5)$

....

88

Rearranging Formulas

Rearranging is getting the letter you want out of the
formula and making it the subject.

Remember
The same method applies
to rearranging formulas
as solving equations

Q1 Rearrange the following formulas to make the <u>letter in brackets</u> the new subject:

a) $y = x + 4$ (x)

d) $a = 7b + 10$ (b)

g) $y = 3x + \frac{1}{2}$ (x)

....

....

....

b) $y = 2x + 3$ (x)

e) $w = 14 + 2z$ (z)

h) $y = 3 - x$ (x)

....

....

....

c) $y = 4x - 5$ (x)

f) $s = 4t - 3$ (t)

i) $y = 5(x + 2)$ (x)

....

....

....

Q2 Rearrange the following, to make the <u>letter in brackets</u> the subject of the formulas:

a) $y = \frac{x}{10}$ (x) ....

e) $f = \frac{3g}{8}$ (g) ....

b) $s = \frac{t}{14}$ (t) ....

f) $y = \frac{x}{5} + 1$ (x) ....

c) $a = \frac{2b}{3}$ (b) ....

g) $y = \frac{x}{2} - 3$ (x) ....

d) $d = \frac{3e}{4}$ (e) ....

h) $a = \frac{b}{3} - 5$ (b) ....

Q3 A car sales person is paid £w for working m months
and selling c cars, where $w = 500m + 50c$.
a) Rearrange the formula to make <u>c the subject</u>. ....
b) Find the number of cars the sales person sells
in 11 months if he earns £12,100 during that time. ....

Q4 The rectangle has length l cm and width w cm. Its perimeter is p cm.

a) Write down a <u>formula</u>
with p as the subject. ....

b) Rearrange this to make l the subject. ....

c) Find the length of a rectangle of
width 7.5 cm and perimeter 44 cm. ....

UNIT THREE

Trial and Improvement

Q1 Use the trial and improvement method to solve the equation $x^3 = 50$.
Give your answer to one decimal place. Two trials have been done for you.

Try $x = 3$ $x^3 = 27$ (too small)
Try $x = 4$ $x^4 = 64$ (too big)

....

Q2 Use the trial and improvement method to solve these equations.
Give your answers to one decimal place.

a) $x^2 + x = 80$

....

b) $x^3 - x = 100$

....

**Show all the numbers you've tried, not just your final answer...
or you'll be chucking away easy marks.**

Inequalities

Yet another one of those bits of Maths that looks worse than it is —
these are just like equations, really, except for the symbols.

The 4 Inequality Symbols:

> means greater than   < means less than
⩾ means greater than or equal to   ⩽ means less than or equal to

Inequalities can be represented on number lines. You need to know this notation, too:

Eg

number line from -4 to 4 with filled circle at -3 and open circle at 2

represents the inequality $-3 \leqslant x < 2$

REMEMBER:
● includes the value
○ does not include it

Q1 Write down an inequality for each of the diagrams below.

a) number line -1 to 5, filled circle at 0 to filled circle at 4 ....

g) number line -3 to 3, open circle at 0 to open circle at 2 ....

b) number line -2 to 4, filled circle at -1 to open circle at 3 ....

h) number line -17 to -11, filled circle at -15 to filled circle at -14 ....

c) number line 8 to 14, open circle at 9 to filled circle at 13 ....

i) number line 20 to 26, open circle at 25 with arrow right ....

d) number line -4 to 2, open circle at -3 to open circle at 1 ....

j) number line -2 to 4, open circle at -1 to filled circle at 3 ....

e) number line -7 to -1, filled circle at -4 with arrow right ....

k) number line -1 to 5, open circle at 0 to open circle at 5 ....

f) number line 0 to 6, arrow left with open circle at 5 ....

l) number line -3 to 3, arrow left with open circle at 1 ....

Q2 Solve the following inequalities:

a) $2x \geqslant 16$ ....

b) $4x > -20$ ....

c) $x + 2 > 5$ ....

d) $x - 3 \leqslant 10$ ....

e) $x + 4 \geqslant 14$ ....

f) $10x > -2$ ....

g) $5 + x \geqslant 12$ ....

h) $x/4 > 10$ ....

i) $x/3 \leqslant 1$ ....

j) $x/2 \leqslant 4$ ....

k) $5x + 4 < 24$ ....

l) $5x + 7 \leqslant 32$ ....

m) $3x + 12 \leqslant 30$ ....

n) $2x - 7 \geqslant 8$ ....

o) $17 + 4x < 33$ ....

Q3 There are <u>1,130</u> pupils in a school and no classes have
more than <u>32</u> pupils. How many <u>classrooms</u> could be
used? Show this information as an inequality.

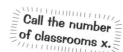

Call the number
of classrooms x.

....

Gradients of Lines

The gradient of a line is just a measure of the slope.
The box below tells you everything you need to know about it...

Finding the Gradient of a line

Gradient of line AB = $\dfrac{\text{y-coordinate of B} - \text{y-coordinate of A}}{\text{x-coordinate of B} - \text{x-coordinate of A}}$

A' (4,2)

'Downhill' gradients are always <u>negative</u>

B' (7,1)

Gradient of line A'B' = $\dfrac{1-2}{7-4} = -\dfrac{1}{3}$

B (4,5)

'Uphill' gradients are always <u>positive</u>

A (2,1)

Gradient of line AB = $\dfrac{5-1}{4-2} = \dfrac{4}{2} = 2$

Midpoint of line AB = (average of x-coords, average of y-coords)

Midpoint of line AB = $\left(\dfrac{4+2}{2}, \dfrac{5+1}{2}\right) = (3,3)$

Q1 Draw axes with x from -9 to 9 and y from -12 to 12. On this set of axes join each <u>pair of points</u> and work out the <u>gradient</u> and the <u>midpoint</u> of the line.

A is (1, 1), B is (2, 4)

gradient of AB = ...

midpoint of AB = ...

C is (5, 5), D is (7, 0)

gradient of CD = ...

midpoint of CD = ...

E is (-7, 7), F is (-2, 10)

gradient of EF = ...

midpoint of EF = ...

G is (-6, 2), H is (-3,-4)

gradient of GH = ...

midpoint of GH = ...

I is (-8,-9), J is (-3,-6)

gradient of IJ = ...   midpoint of IJ = ...

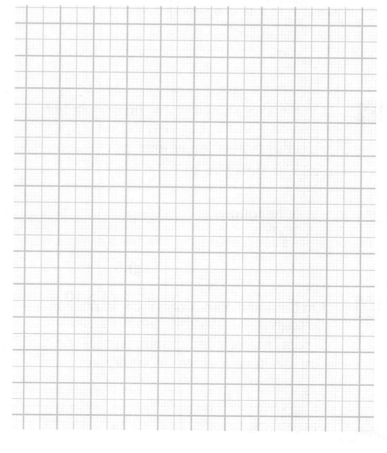

92

Finding the Equation of a Straight Line

 Now you know how to find the gradient, you can go
a couple of steps further and find the equation of a line.

STEP 1: Work out the gradient of the line, call this 'm'.

STEP 2: Find where the graph crosses the y-axis, call this 'c',

STEP 3: Put your values into the formula y = mx + c — and that's it!

Q1 For each of these lines, find the gradient, m, and the y-intercept, c.
Hence write down the <u>equation</u> of the line.

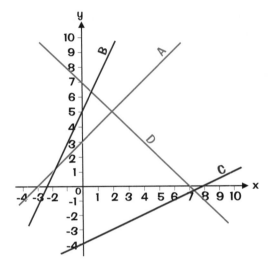

Line A:

m = ..., c = ...

equation is ....

Line B:

m = ..., c = ...

equation is ....

Line C:

m = ..., c = ...

equation is ....

Line D:

m = ..., c = ...

equation is ....

Q2 On the axes shown, draw the <u>straight line</u>
which passes through A(1, 2) and B(5, 4).
Find its gradient (m), y-intercept (c) and
use this to write down its equation.

c = ..., m = ...

equation is ....

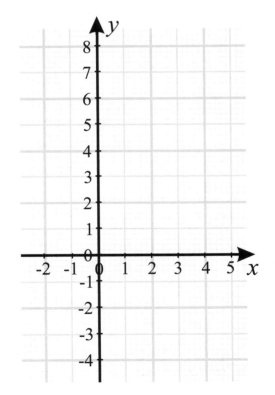

Q3 On the same axes, draw the line passing
through points P (-2,-4) and Q (4, 8).
Find its gradient (m), y-intercept (c) and
use this to write down its equation.

c = ..., m = ...

equation is ....

UNIT THREE

Simultaneous Equations with Graphs

The solution of two simultaneous equations is simply the X and Y values where their graphs cross

1) Simultaneous equations can be plotted as two <u>straight-line graphs</u> on the <u>same axes</u>.

2) The point where the lines cross will have <u>coordinates</u> equal to the <u>values of x and y</u> which satisfy both equations.

Eg: Solve:
$$y = x + 1$$
$$2y + x = 14$$

The two lines <u>intersect</u> where <u>x = 4</u> and <u>y = 5</u>, so this is the solution.

Q1 Solve these simultaneous equations by looking at the graphs.
Then check your answers by substituting the values back into the equations.

a) $y + 2x = 9$
$3y = x + 6$

Solution:
x = ..., y = ...

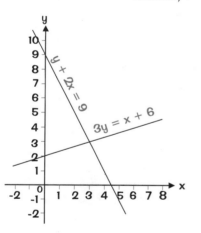

c) $y = x + 6$
$3y + x = 18$

Solution:
x = ..., y = ...

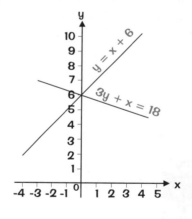

b) $y = 2x + 14$
$2y = 8 - x$

Solution:
x = ..., y = ...

Check your answers in the equations even if you're not asked to.

d) $y + x = 1$
$3y = x + 11$

Solution:
x = ..., y = ...

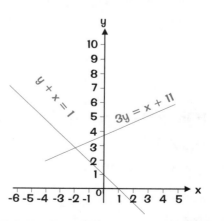

UNIT THREE

Quadratic Graphs

If an expression has an x^2 term in it, it is quadratic. The graphs you get from quadratic expressions are always curves with a certain shape...

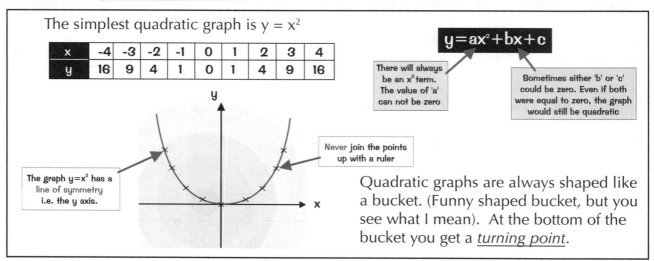

The simplest quadratic graph is $y = x^2$

x	-4	-3	-2	-1	0	1	2	3	4
y	16	9	4	1	0	1	4	9	16

$$y = ax^2 + bx + c$$

There will always be an x^2 term. The value of 'a' can not be zero

Sometimes either 'b' or 'c' could be zero. Even if both were equal to zero, the graph would still be quadratic

Never join the points up with a ruler

The graph $y=x^2$ has a line of symmetry i.e. the y axis.

Quadratic graphs are always shaped like a bucket. (Funny shaped bucket, but you see what I mean). At the bottom of the bucket you get a *turning point*.

You'll need some graph paper for the questions on this page.

Q1 Complete this <u>table of values</u> for the quadratic graph $y = 2x^2$.

a) On your graph paper, draw axes with x from -4 to 4 and y from 0 to 32.

b) Plot these 9 points and join them with a <u>smooth curve</u>.

x	-4	-3	-2	-1	0	1	2	3	4
$y=2x^2$	32	18					8		

Remember to square first then x 2

Q2 Complete this table of values for the graph $y = x^2 + x$.

x	-4	-3	-2	-1	0	1	2	3	4
x^2	16	9					4		
$y=x^2+x$	12					2			

By putting more steps in your table of values, the arithmetic is easier

a) Draw axes with x from -4 to 4 and y from 0 to 20.
b) Plot the points and join them with a smooth curve.
c) Draw the <u>line of symmetry</u> for the quadratic graph $y = x^2 + x$, and label it.
d) Use your graph to find the two solutions of the equation $x^2 + x = 0$.

x = ... or ....

Just find the x-values where the graph crosses the x-axis (i.e. where y = 0).

If the x^2 term has a <u>minus</u> sign in front of it, the bucket will be turned <u>upside down</u>.

Q3 **a)** Draw the graph $y = -x^2 + x + 4$ for values of x from -3 to 4.
b) Use your graph to find approximate solutions to the equation $-x^2 + x + 4 = 0$

x = ... or ....

Interpreting Graphs

Q1 Using the <u>conversion graph</u> convert the following to km, rounding your answers to the <u>nearest km</u>:

a) 5 miles ....   **c)** 11 miles ....

b) 20 miles ....   **d)** 23 miles ....

Q2 Change the following to <u>miles</u>, rounding your answers to the nearest mile:

a) 10 km ....   **c)** 27 km ....

b) 20 km ....   **d)** 35 km ....

Q3 Match the following graphs with the statements below:

a) The cost of hiring a plumber <u>per hour</u> including a <u>fixed call-out fee</u>. ....

b) <u>Exchange rate</u> between Euros and American Dollars. ....

c) <u>Speed against time</u> for a car travelling at constant speed. ....

d) The <u>area of a circle</u> as the radius increases. ....

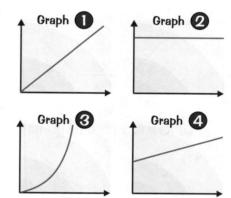

Q4 The graph shows Nicola's car journey from her house to Alan's house, picking up Robbie on the way.

a) If Nicola started her trip at 10.00 am at what time did she return home? ....

b) How far is Robbie's house from Nicola's? ....

c) How long did they stop at Alan's for? ....

d) During which section was the speed greatest? ....

e) How long did the return journey take? ....

f) What was the speed of the car during section E? ....

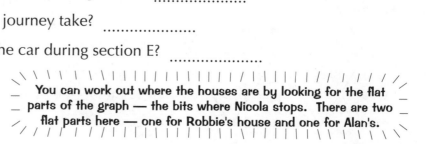

You can work out where the houses are by looking for the flat parts of the graph — the bits where Nicola stops. There are two flat parts here — one for Robbie's house and one for Alan's.

96

Regular Polygons

You need to remember these two formulas for polygons:

Sum of Exterior angles = 360°

and **Sum of Interior angles = (n – 2) × 180°**

(n is the number of sides)

Interior angle

Exterior angle

Q1 Here is a regular octagon:

a) What is the total of its eight interior angles? ....

b) What is the size of the marked angle? ....

Here is a regular pentagon:

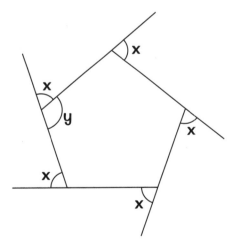

c) The five angles marked x are its exterior angles. What do they add up to?

....

d) Work out the value of x.

....

e) Use your answer from part **d)** to work out the value of angle y.

....

Q2 The diagram shows a regular hexagon:

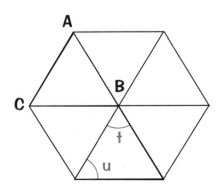

a) Work out the size of angles t and u.

....

b) What type of triangle is ABC? ....

UNIT THREE

Pythagoras' Theorem

If you're as big a fan of Pythagoras as me, you'll ignore him and use this method instead:

h(hypotenuse)

b

$a^2 + b^2 = h^2$

a

The Simple Three Step Method
1) SQUARE the two numbers that you are given.
2) To find the <u>longest side, ADD</u> the two squared numbers. To find a <u>shorter side, SUBTRACT</u> the smaller one from the larger.
3) Take the SQUARE ROOT. Then check that your answer is sensible.

Q1 Using Pythagoras' theorem, calculate the length of the third side in these triangles, giving your answers to <u>3 significant figures</u>.

$c^2 =$ .... $+$ .... $=$ ...., $c =$ ....

$d^2 =$ .... $+$ .... $=$ ...., $d =$ ....

$e^2 =$ .... $-$ .... $=$ ...., $e =$ ....

$f^2 =$ .... $-$ .... $=$ ...., $f =$ ....

Q2 Using Pythagoras' theorem, work out which of these triangles have right-angles.

If they don't have right-angles, the numbers won't fit the formula.

....

....

Q3 Calculate the <u>missing lengths</u> in these quadrilaterals. Give your answers to 3 sig. figs.

h = ..., i = ...,

j = ..., k = ...,

l = ..., m = ...

The Circle Formulas

Q1   Calculate the area of each circle.
Write your answers to **a)** and **b)** as multiples of π.

a)

2cm

Area = π × radius² = ...

b) A circle of radius 9 cm.   Area = π × radius² = ...

Give your answers to **c)** and **d)** to 3 sig. figs.

c)

11cm

You must find the radius first.

Radius = diameter / 2 = ...

Area = ...

d) A circle of diameter 28 cm.   Radius = ...

Area = ...

Q2   Find the area of one face of a 10p coin, radius 1.2 cm.
Give your answer correct to 3 sig. figs.

Area = ...

Q3   A circular table has a diameter of 50 cm.
Find the circumference and area of the table to 3 sig. figs.

Circumference = ...   Area = ...

Q4   What is the area of this semicircular rug?
Give your answer to the nearest whole number.

150cm

Area = ...

Q5   The circumference of a circle is 195 cm.
Calculate its diameter correct to 3 sig. figs.

Diameter = ...

Q6   This circular pond has a circular path around it. The radius of the pond is 72 m and the
path is 2 m wide. Calculate to the nearest whole number:

path

pond

the area of the pond ....

the area of the path ....

Loci and Constructions

You've gotta be ultra neat with these — you'll lose easy marks if your pictures are scruffy — and let's face it, you'd rather have them, wouldn't you.

Constructions should always be done as accurately as possible using:

sharp pencil, ruler, compasses, protractor (set-square).

Q1 a) Draw a circle with radius 4 cm.

Draw in a diameter of the circle. Label one end of the diameter X and the other end Y.

Mark a point somewhere on the circumference — not too close to X or Y. Label your point T. Join X to T and T to Y.

The middle letter is where the angle is.

Measure angle XTY.   Angle XTY = ...°

b) Make an accurate drawing below of the triangle on the right. Measure side AB on your triangle, giving your answer in millimetres.

AB = ... mm

Loci and Constructions

Work through these questions bit by bit, and remember the following...

LOCUS — a line showing all points obeying the given rule.
BISECTOR — a line splitting an angle or line exactly in two.

Q2 Two churches with bell towers are 2 km apart. On a still day, the sound of the bells can be heard 1.5 km away. To the right, draw an accurate diagram to show the two churches, and for each one, draw the locus of points where its bell can be heard. Shade the area where <u>both</u> bells can be heard.

Q3 **a)** In the space to the left, construct a triangle ABC with AB = 4 cm, BC = 5 cm, AC = 3 cm.

b) Construct the perpendicular bisector of AB and where this line meets BC, label the new point D.

Q4 Tony likes to look at the tree in his garden. The diagram to the right shows the position of the tree relative to his bedroom window. Tony wants to position his bed in such a way that he can see the tree in the morning as he awakes.

Carefully <u>shade</u> on the diagram the area in which Tony could position his bed.

He doesn't need to be able to see the whole tree.

Symmetry

 To work out if you've got a line of symmetry, just imagine you're folding the shape in half. If the sides will fold exactly together, then hey presto, it's symmetrical about the fold.

Q1 These shapes have more than one line of symmetry.
Draw the lines of symmetry using dotted lines.

a)   **b)**   **c)**

Q2 Some of the letters of the alphabet have lines of symmetry.
Draw the lines of symmetry using dotted lines.

A B C D E F G H I J K L M

N O P Q R S T U V W X Y Z

Q3 Write down the order of rotational symmetry of each of the following shapes:

a)
square

b)
rectangle

c)
equilateral triangle

d)
parallelogram

Q4 Complete the following diagrams so that they have rotational symmetry about centre C of the order stated:

a) order 2   **b)** order 4   **c)** order 3

      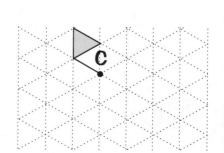

Symmetry

Q5 Which of the following shaded planes are planes of symmetry?

A   B   C

....

Q6 Give 6 examples of a plane of symmetry for a cube:
(The first one is done for you)

Q7 A tessellation is a pattern made with identical 2-D shapes which fit together exactly leaving no gaps. Continue these tessellations.

Planes of symmetry are a bit of a pain to draw, but if you shade them in a different colour from the rest of the object they'll be a lot easier to see.

Transformations — Translation

Translations can be described using <u>vectors</u>.

The vector $\begin{pmatrix} 2 \\ 5 \end{pmatrix}$ means move 2 spaces to the <u>right</u> and 5 spaces <u>up</u>.

The vector $\begin{pmatrix} -3 \\ -4 \end{pmatrix}$ means move 3 spaces to the <u>left</u> and 4 spaces <u>down</u>.

Q1 Translate the shapes A, B and C using these vectors: A $\begin{pmatrix} -4 \\ -3 \end{pmatrix}$ B $\begin{pmatrix} 5 \\ 5 \end{pmatrix}$ C $\begin{pmatrix} 4 \\ -4 \end{pmatrix}$
Label the images A', B' and C'.

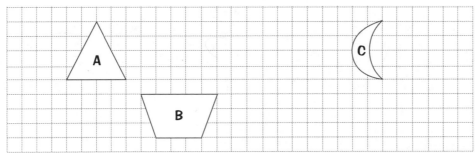

Q2 Translate shape A below using the vectors given in order, drawing the image each time:

P $\begin{pmatrix} 3 \\ 4 \end{pmatrix}$ Q $\begin{pmatrix} 9 \\ 2 \end{pmatrix}$

R $\begin{pmatrix} 3 \\ -4 \end{pmatrix}$ S $\begin{pmatrix} -8 \\ -4 \end{pmatrix}$

Label the images
A', A'', A''', A''''.

Q3 Write down the <u>translation vectors</u> for the translations shown.

  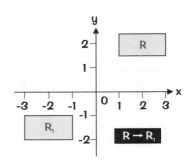

a) .... b) .... c) ....

104

Transformations — Reflection

Q1 Reflect each shape in the line x = 4.

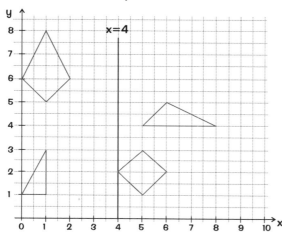

Q2 Reflect the shapes in the line y = x.

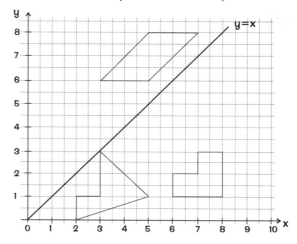

Q3 Reflect ① in the line y = 5, label this ②.

Reflect ② in the line x = 9, label this ③.

Reflect ③ in the line y = x, label this ④.

Reflect ④ in the line x = 4, label this ⑤.

Reflect ⑤ in the line y = x, label this ⑥.

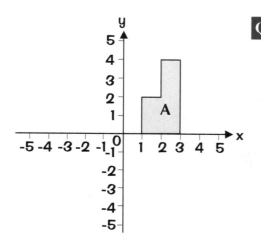

Q4

a) Draw the result of reflecting shape A in the <u>x-axis</u>, label this A′.

b) Draw the result of reflecting shape A′ in the <u>y-axis</u>, label this A″.

c) What <u>single transformation</u> would turn shape A into shape A″?

....

Nothing fancy here, is there? Reflection's just mirror drawing really.
And we've all done that before...

Transformations — Rotation

Q1 The centre of rotation for each of these diagrams is **X**. Rotate (turn) each shape as asked then draw the new position of the shape onto each of the diagrams below.

a) 180° (or ½ turn).

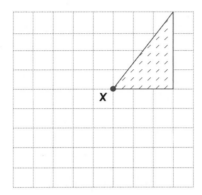

b) 270° anticlockwise (or ¾ turn anticlockwise).

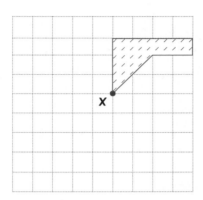

Q2 This is a scalene triangle PQR. The centre of rotation is the origin 0.

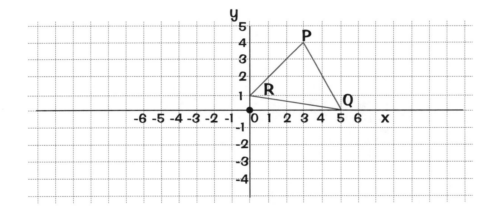

a) Write down the coordinates of...

P .... Q .... R ....

b) Rotate the triangle 90° anticlockwise about the origin 0.
Label the new triangle P′ Q′ R′.

c) Write down the coordinates of ...

P′ .... Q′ .... R′ ....

A _½ turn clockwise_ is the same as a _½ turn anti-clockwise_ — and a _¼ turn clockwise_ is the same as a _¾ turn anti-clockwise_. Great fun, innit...

UNIT THREE

Transformations — Enlargement

The scale factor is a fancy way of saying **HOW MUCH BIGGER** the enlargement is than the original. If it's less than 1, it's a reduction. A scale factor of 1/3 means it's reduced to a third of the original size.

Q1 What is the scale factor of each of these enlargements?

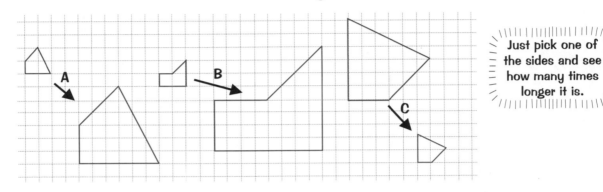

Just pick one of the sides and see how many times longer it is.

A: Scale factor is .... **B:** Scale factor is .... **C:** Scale factor is ....

Q2 Enlarge this triangle using scale factor 4 and centre of enlargement C.

Q3 a) Enlarge this shape using scale factor 3 and centre of enlargement E.

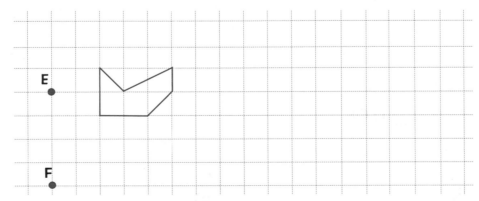

b) Now enlarge the original shape using scale factor 0.5 and centre of enlargement F.

Careful — this is actually a reduction.

Similarity and Enlargement

Similarity and Scale Factor

Two shapes are <u>similar</u> if they're the <u>same shape</u> but different size. The lengths of the two shapes are related to the scale factor by this very important formula triangle:

Q1 Two picture frames are shown. One picture is <u>similar</u> to the other. Calculate L cm, the length of the smaller frame.

....

Q2 For each of the following pairs, say with a reason whether the shapes are similar.

i)

iii)

....

ii)

iv)

....

Q3 Angle ABC = Angle PQR and Angle BCA = Angle QRP

a) Are the triangles similar? ....

Calculate the following lengths:

b) AB .... **c)** QR ....

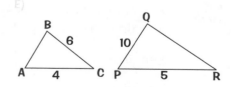

Q4 Which of the following must be <u>similar</u> to each other? ....

A Two circles   **C** Two rectangles   **E** Two equilateral triangles

B Two rhombuses   **D** Two squares   **F** Two isosceles triangles

UNIT THREE

Scale Drawings

Watch out for those units... there's quite a mixture here —
you'll have to convert some of them before you can go anywhere.

Q1 A rectangular room measures 20 m long and 15 m wide. Work out the measurements
for a scale drawing of the room using a scale of 1 cm = 2 m.

Length = ... Width = ...

Q2 Katie drew a scale drawing of the top of her
desk. She used a scale of 1:10. This is her
drawing of the computer keyboard. What
are the actual dimensions of it?

Length = ... Width = ...

Q3 This is a scale drawing of Paul's new car.
Measure the length of the car. .... cm.

If the drawing uses a scale of 1 : 90,
work out the actual length of the car.

....

Q4 A rectangular field is 60 m long and 40 m wide. The farmer needs to make a scale
drawing of it. He uses a scale of 1 : 2000. Work out the measurements for the scale
drawing. (Hint — change the m to cm.)

....

....

Q5 A rectangular room is 4.8 m long and 3.6 m wide. Make a scale drawing of it using
a scale of 1 cm to 120 cm. First work out the measurements for the scale drawing.

Length = ...

Width = ...

On your scale drawing mark a window, whose
actual length is 2.4 m, on one long wall and mark
a door, actual width 90 cm, on one short wall.

Window = ...

Door = ...